# MODES AND MANNERS

# MODES AND MANNERS

*By* Max von Boehn
*Translated by* Joan Joshua

MAGDALENA, COUNTESS OF PFALZ-NEUBURG

Peter Candid

*Fr.*                    *Art Gallery, Schleissheim*

# MODES AND MANNERS

BY
## MAX VON BOEHN

TRANSLATED BY
## JOAN JOSHUA

VOLUME III
## THE SEVENTEENTH CENTURY

*Illustrated with Reproductions of
Contemporary Paintings etc.*

## GEORGE G. HARRAP & CO. LTD.
LONDON      BOMBAY      SYDNEY

*First published* 1935
*by* GEORGE G. HARRAP & CO. LTD.
182 *High Holborn, London, W.C.*1

MADE IN GREAT BRITAIN. PRINTED AT THE PITMAN PRESS, BATH

# FOREWORD

THE author, working on similar lines to those followed in the earlier volumes of the series, has also in this volume made use of works of art of a given period to depict the contemporary world of fashion. Thus the illustrations have been selected throughout from authentic seventeenth-century material, arranged as far as possible in strict chronological order. Wherever the original paintings and engravings bear a date, or some other positive evidence of this is forthcoming, it has been added to the legend. Among these illustrations with definite dates have been inserted others whose period can only be approximately gauged. In such cases there is always a certain risk of error, but readers acquainted with the difficulties of the material will examine the work with indulgence, realizing that when all is said and done it is quite excusable to misdate a portrait by ten or even by twenty or thirty years.

Both the author and the publishers take this opportunity of expressing their gratitude for the reception accorded to the work, and of acknowledging the kind help in the compilation of the present volume of the heads of the Print Room of the Berlin Museums, the Kaiser-Friedrich Museum, the Museum of Art and Industry, and the Lipperheide Library of Costume, in Berlin, of the Collection of Graphic Art, the Alte Pinakothek, and the National Museum of Bavaria, in Munich, and of the Art Gallery at Schleissheim.

MAX VON BOEHN

# TRANSLATOR'S NOTE

I MUST express my deep regret that the author, Herr Max von Boehn, who gave me such kind help in the translation of the two volumes of this series published in 1932, has since passed away.

Since the original work, wide though its scope, was naturally compiled primarily for a German public, I have sought to increase its value for the English reader, first, by the insertion of editorial footnotes, for all of which I must assume responsibility; and, secondly, by expressing sums of money in British currency wherever the author gave sufficient data to enable the conversion of seventeenth-century values into modern (1914) values or supplied these values himself. Some slight inaccuracies in the text have been amended, but in a number of cases of doubtful or erroneous statement the correction of which would have involved disturbance of the context I have contented myself with the insertion of a cautionary *sic*. The descriptions of illustrations have been brought, where possible, up to date, and references to the illustrations inserted in the text where considered useful.

As the systematic Anglicizing of proper names would only have deprived them in great part of the flavour of their nationality and period, the method has been adopted of leaving the names of little-known persons in their native form, while employing in the case of foreigners of high rank or repute either English equivalents or forms familiar to English people.

For the basis of some of the notes and amendments I am in great part indebted to *A History of German Literature* (1931), by Professor J. G. Robertson, to *Historic Costume* (second edition, 1929), by Francis M. Kelly and Randolph Schwabe, and to *Das Kostüm der Blütezeit Hollands, 1600–60* (1930), by Frithjof van Thienen.

JOAN JOSHUA

7

# CONTENTS

# ILLUSTRATIONS

## PLATES IN COLOUR

11

# MODES AND MANNERS

## ILLUSTRATIONS IN THE TEXT

# ILLUSTRATIONS

# MODES AND MANNERS

14

# ILLUSTRATIONS

# MODES AND MANNERS

# MODES AND MANNERS

## CHAPTER I
### GENERAL CONDITIONS

T HE schism created by Luther's Reformation divided the Christian world into two hostile camps which filled with the din of their conflicts not only the sixteenth but the seventeenth century. The longer these conflicts lasted the more bitter they became, but the more, on the other hand, was their original nature submerged. Dissensions which had at the outset been purely religious in spirit became tinged with so many worldly motives, disputes over dogmatic trivialities came finally to be entangled with so many questions of political power, that the religious wars of the seventeenth century acquired an entirely different character from those of the sixteenth. Although the Thirty Years War has been called "the last great religious war," [1] it is questionable whether it may rightly be termed one at all. What a truly remarkable religious war, in which the sympathies of the Pope are displayed on the side of the Swedish monarch, in which a Cardinal of the Church of Rome, first Minister of his Most Christian Catholic Majesty, goes to the aid of the German Lutherans, and in which the army of Wallenstein, Imperial commander-in-chief, is composed almost entirely of Protestants and will tolerate no Catholic priest within its ranks! Magdeburg would never have been vanquished by Tilly [2] had not the Protestant merchants of Hamburg supplied the Imperial troops with munitions. The Bohemian nobility who gave the final spur to this war

The Thirty Years War

---

[1] Henry Thomas Buckle, *Introduction to the History of Civilization in England* (1904 edition), p. 309.
[2] Count von Tilly, general of the Catholic League, rose to fame after his victory in the battle of the White Mountain (see p. 107, *n.* 2) over the forces of Frederick, Count Palatine, head of the Evangelical Union.

by electing as king of Bohemia Frederick, Count Palatine, were swayed less by religious motives than by the desire to augment their particular rights and privileges; when they had nothing further to gain from the ruler of their choice they promptly forsook him. And just as the Thirty Years War in Germany was a struggle between the power of the Emperor and of the princes, for which adherence to a Church

HENRY IV OF FRANCE AND HIS FAMILY
Léonard Gaultier. 1602

was only a pretext, so the civil wars of this century in France and England also partook of a political character. The French Huguenots, even after they had enjoyed complete toleration for many years, and when the highest offices both of State and at court were in the hands of their party, remained a stumbling-block to political unity; and the antagonism existing between the English Protestants and their Catholic or catholicizing rulers hinged in reality far more upon politics than beliefs. While the Stuarts openly or in secret upheld the Catholic Church because they regarded it as the tool of despotism, the Protestants championed democratic freedom. Although the two parties took their names and watchwords

QUEEN ELIZABETH
Crispin van de Passe

from their religious antitheses, they were merely fighting for power in the name of faith.

Glancing in retrospect over more than a century of national

warfare waged ostensibly for freedom of faith, it becomes evident that in the course of the conflict the issues at stake had changed: the differences between Catholics and Protestants no longer loomed so large, for in the meantime the day of absolutism had arrived. In Germany, in place of a central Government, arose the autonomous power of the ruling princes, which placed men under a very different yoke from that of religious belief, for it brought bureaucracy and standing armies in its train. Although faith still formed the subject of heated dispute, it signified far less now, for the whole order of society had changed and obeyed new laws. The old medieval distinction between nobility, middle class, and peasantry still existed, but the mutual relationship of these classes had undergone a gradual change. The peasant had been pushed yet lower down the scale, and under the yoke of a merciless bondage was condemned to a barely human existence. The middle class, on the other hand, had risen in life, for it was on all sides attaining to posts among a steadily increasing body of officials where efficiency and knowledge were required. When in England it succeeded in crushing tyranny and the Habeas Corpus Act was passed[1]—the first law securing the freedom of the subject from the arbitrary powers of ruler, nobility, and clergy—this class acquired lasting esteem. Gratitude is undoubtedly due to the English middle class for having made progress possible in the world.

The greatest change witnessed in the seventeenth century, however, was that suffered by the nobility;[2] but if their prestige was less the outward show they made was correspondingly greater. What a striking contrast between those aristocrats who still could attempt to depose Louis XIII from the throne and their successors, whose highest honour consisted in attending the levee of Louis XIV! At the start of the century the nobles prided themselves upon

The Nobility

[1] This Act became law in 1679.
[2] In Germany, in the seventeenth century, this description was usually applied to persons of Imperial estate below the rank of a prince. The Imperial estates privileged to a seat and vote in the Reichstag then were (a) ecclesiastical estates, (b) temporal estates—i.e., electors, dukes, princes, landgraves, waldgraves, burgraves, counts, and barons of the realm.

A DANCING-PARTY

Crispin van de Passe

their power, at its close upon their titles; at one time dignity and self-esteem sprang from within them; now they sought it at court. A variety of factors contributed to this change. For one thing, as the result of interminable warfare the nobility were seriously impoverished, but a still more potent cause lay in the unbounded public idolatry which accom-

panied the growing power of the princes. In the eyes of the people every court was a supreme earthly paradise, each ruler a superhuman being. Even so insignificant a princeling as Ernest Ludwig of Hesse was thus addressed by a political writer: "If God were not God, who should more properly be God than your Serene Highness?" The princes stood not only above the law, but outside all codes of ethics and morality; they came, in fact, next in order to God. Small wonder, then, that any connexion with them, even

DRAWING BY HENDRIK GOLTZIUS
*Print Room of the Berlin Museums*

in the capacity of servant, was prized as the highest honour to which men could aspire. The voluntary abandonment by the aristocracy of their former freedom and their consequent degradation from equality with the princes to the rank of subjects—to no better, indeed, than lackeys—was accompanied by a growth in their numbers which could only lower their prestige. The Emperor Ferdinand II alone created thirty new princes, seventy counts, and a hundred barons of the realm, and under his successors the increase was so rapid that Princess Charlotte of the Palatinate, for one, never wearied of poking fun at the new German nobility. In 1680 Sophia, Electress of Hanover, writes, "Titles are

PORTRAIT OF A LADY
Unknown master
*Von Lipperheide Library of Costume, Berlin*
22

certainly waxing apace in the kingdom, but power and prosperity are waning." In order to maintain the balance of power against a rebellious aristocracy of ancient lineage,

THE ARTIST AND HIS FIRST WIFE, ISABELLA BRANT
Peter Paul Rubens. 1610
*Photo F. Bruckmann A.-G., Munich*

King Frederick of Denmark [1] created a new nobility with new grades; and Charles II of England and Louis XIV of France gave all their illegitimate sons titles which raised them far above the ranks of the old aristocracy. Louis XIV, indeed,

[1] Frederick III.

owing to the repeated financial embarrassments of his Government, actually made ennoblement compulsory; in 1695 five hundred titles, each costing six thousand livres,[1] had to be acquired by wealthy *bourgeois*. This course proved most disastrous in Germany, which since the Peace of Münster and Osnabrück had possessed some eighteen hundred territorial

CHRISTIAN OVERSCHIE OF DELFT
Johannes Wierx

lords, over three hundred of whom took care at least to have their say at the permanent Diet at Ratisbon, since action was now beside the question. It was at the court-households of these petty rulers that this rage for honours was fostered, for there the practice was initiated of conferring court appointments upon artisans and craftsmen, thus helping to spread still more widely the habit of judging by externals.

Although the partitioning of the Empire into nearly two thousand units frittered away its strength and the triviality of the system brought ridicule upon the princes and their retinues, the fact that this multitude of small courts acted to some degree as centres of culture may perhaps be regarded as one favourable factor in the face of many adverse ones. Not that they made any attempt to encourage the fine arts or to patronize literature, but they did assist to some extent in restoring to a people impoverished and brutalized by the depredations of a prolonged war a sense of greater refinement—even if such refinement remained for a long time confined to externals.

Such was the misery inflicted upon Germany by the Thirty Years War that the civilization of this unfortunate country was thrown back for generations behind that of its more

[1] For the value of the livre see p. 138, *n.* 3.

CARICATURE OF THE FARTHINGALE AND THE MASK
1610

prosperous neighbours. The conclusion of peace[1] found it poorer by one-half, some authorities say by two-thirds or even three-quarters, of its former population. Of 400,000 inhabitants of Württemberg only 48,000, of three million in Bohemia only 780,000, remained; in 1648 the citizens of Berlin numbered no more than 300, at Hirschberg they had dwindled from 900 to 60, and out of 80,000 Augsburg had lost 62,000. Already by 1636 the peasants in the Rhenish Palatinate are said to have totalled a bare two hundred; in Saxony, within two years alone, 900,000 souls had perished, with the result that by the end of the war 343 communes in the Saxon Electorate lay deserted, eighty of these being in the district of Wittenberg alone. In Bavaria a hundred villages and in Hesse three hundred presented scenes of complete desolation, while in the Ruppin area only four villages were left standing. In Brandenburg and Silesia the wild animals outnumbered the peasants. "One may wander ten miles," writes the author of the *Excidium Germaniæ* [*sic*], "without setting eyes on either cattle or man." Whole farmsteads were leased for no greater consideration than obligatory services. And Germany suffered a diminution of fortune as immeasurable as her sacrifice in souls. As early as 1634 Duke Frederick William of Brunswick estimated the financial losses of his province at eighty million gulden, and between the years 1628 and 1650 Württemberg had to meet war levies totalling 118 million. Wallenstein and Montecuccoli[2] succeeded in extorting from the Kurmark[3] twenty million thalers; Leipzig estimated its war indemnities at 1,075,250 thalers; Wismar—quite a small town—had to contribute 170,000 thalers, Esslingen two million gulden within five years, Goslar 544,000 thalers in a year.[4] When Wallenstein subdued Silesia burghers and peasants were called upon to

Depopulation and Poverty

[1] The Thirty Years War ended in 1648.

[2] Count von Raimondo, prince of the Holy Roman Empire and an Austrian general.

[3] A part of the Mark of Brandenburg.

[4] After the disappearance of the gold gulden in Germany toward the middle of the seventeenth century the silver gulden was worth about two-thirds of a thaler, which averaged between 1*s.* 6*d.* and 2*s.* 6*d.* The ducat was then worth about 9.6 marks, or 9*s.* 7*d.*

surrender one-half, the nobility and bureaucracy two-thirds of their income. During the years 1628–31 Blankenburg-in-the-Harz was occupied by Imperial troops, and had to find several thousand thalers a month. As the deserted and trampled fields yielded no harvests, famines ensued, all but exterminating the enfeebled population. By 1634 a bushel of corn in Bavaria was worth twenty gulden, and when the Swedish army was quartered in the Duchy of Gotha in 1640 a loaf of bread there cost a ducat; in 1639 the citizens of Leipzig had to stay their hunger on cats and dogs. According to contemporary reports, not only fallen cattle but even human bodies were disinterred for food, and children were systematically pursued and slaughtered for purposes of consumption. When at the siege of Nördlingen a

DRAWING BY WILLEM P. BUYTEWECH
*Print Room of the Berlin Museums*

tower collapsed and caught fire the starving population flung themselves upon the charred corpses and fought for shreds of their flesh.

The demon of war raged throughout German territory, leaving in its wake destruction, desolation, and a demoralized people. Some, impoverished and enfeebled, had become apathetic; others, grown rich with spoils, stayed coarse and brutish. Heavy losses on the one hand contrasted with colossal gains on the other. The knowledge that Wallenstein's fortune at the time of his dismissal was computed at nine million gulden affords some guide to the whereabouts of the

61,881 gulden of which Count Pückler claimed to have been robbed between 1632 and 1637, nor should it be forgotten

A DUTCH COUPLE
Jacob Matham

A FRENCH COUPLE
Crispin van de Passe

that these seventeenth-century figures must always be multiplied by five for comparison with present-day (1914) values.

DRAWING BY JACOB DE GHEYN
Print Room of the Berlin Museums

When employed in the service of Sweden Count Hohenlohe managed to pocket 117,000 thalers, and the booty amassed by General Königsmarck enabled him to leave his heirs an annual income of 130,000 thalers. No less magnificent were the spoils of men who had risen from the lowest ranks. After the sack of Mantua Count Johann Aldringer, formerly a servingman, placed 800,000 kronen in Venetian banks as his share of the plunder, and the Imperial Count Peter Holzapfel, once a Hessian yokel,

AN EVENING PARTY
Peter Isselburg. 1613

succeeded in amassing a million and a half thalers. In those days a man could do profitable business by selling his estates and devoting the proceeds to founding a regiment. Evidence of this is contained in a letter written to the Emperor in 1629 by Leopold, Archduke of Tirol, in which he laments the fact that any number of officers who were as poor as church mice

YOUNG GALLANTS
Jacques Callot. 1617

when they joined the forces were now the possessors of three or four hundred thousand gulden in cash.

Not just for a handful of years but for many decades the world lived at the point of the sword. The battle was to the bold then, and even as in the first Napoleonic era, so many generations later, a remarkable wave of fortune turned the tide of human affairs, so in the seventeenth century—and not in Germany alone—fate swept to the front men who in the ordinary course of events would never have ventured beyond the modest limits of their particular activities or estates. Poor petty princes like Duke Bernard of Saxe-Weimar, Duke Christian of Brunswick, and Ernst von Mansfeld went to war to gain kingdoms, a policy already pursued with success by Wallenstein; Johann von Werth, a groom, and Derfflinger, a tailor's apprentice, became generals. In

SLEIGHING

Hendrick Averkamp

*Print Room of the Berlin Museums*

BALL AT THE BRUSSELS COURT OF THE ARCHDUKE ALBERT AND THE ARCHDUCHESS ISABELLA
CLARA EUGENIA OF AUSTRIA

Franz Francken the Younger and Franz Pourbus II

*Photo F. Bruckmann A.-G., Munich*

France an equally bellicose spirit reigned; Constable de Luynes,[1] the favourite of Louis XIII, had visions of himself as ruler of a kingdom of Austrasia embracing the districts of Metz, Verdun, and Toul. In England a peasant lad rose to be Lord Protector of the Realm,[2] house-boys to be admirals, and lackeys to be colonels and generals, while tinkers, tailors, and cobblers filled the highest posts in the land [*sic*].

A YOUNG GALLANT
Jacques Callot. 1617

The wars which compassed all this, and which raged in France and England for just as long and with equal violence as in Germany, wrought *Foreign Influence in Germany* more permanent damage in the latter country because they produced far greater changes in its national life. In the English and French civil wars English stood alone against English, French against French. Thanks to their geographical position, these countries were protected against the invasion of foreigners [!], whereas Germany served all the neighbouring nations as a welcome battle-ground. The two great parties warring on German soil positively vied with each other in seeking the services of foreigners. When the Protestants brought in French, Danes, and Swedes on their side the Emperor called Spaniards and Italians to his aid, employed Walloons, and flooded the countryside with wild hordes of semi-barbaric Croats, Magyars, and Slavs; for a time the Radziwills even recruited Cossacks for him. This motley of nationalities left in Germany not only traces of its customs and tongues, but, probably a more radical matter, so much of its stock that after the war the Germans were no longer the same

[1] Charles d'Albert, Duc de Luynes, appointed Constable of France in 1621.
[2] Oliver Cromwell would be described as originally a gentleman-farmer.

THE WEDDING OF ADRIAEN PLOOS VAN AMSTEL AND AGNES VAN BYLER
Willem Cornelisz Duyster. C. 1628

blood, and the predilection for things foreign which it has never quite shaken off may perhaps be regarded as Germany's worst inheritance from the great war. This preference for foreign things, which, although possibly latent, did not really become apparent until during and after the long war, has often been subjected to severe censure by moralists. Germans had already been accused in earlier days of casting an imitative eye across their western borders; never, however, had they shown such a craze for foreign *Kultur* as in the seventeenth century. But, seeing that the political destiny of Germany then lay in the hands of foreign monarchs, is it fair to reproach that time or generation on such a score? It was indeed fortunate that Richelieu prevented the Emperor from subjugating Germany as Louis XIV did France, for a German Empire consolidated under a Catholic Habsburg of the stamp of Ferdinand or Leopold would certainly have sunk to the level of Spain. Owing, however, to the machinations of France and Sweden in the Peace of Westphalia, the German Emperor retained little or no voice within the Empire, and these two countries secured terms which enabled them to interfere repeatedly and with every semblance of right in Germany's internal affairs. Any art produced during this century on German soil revealed Italian influence, but for all other cultural matters the model was supplied by France.

It is in the German language of the century that foreign influence is most apparent. Not until quite recent [pre-War] days have serious attempts been made to expurgate from German the traces left in its words, phraseology, construction, and expressions by the idioms of the nations which congregated on German soil in the course of the Thirty Years War—of practically the whole of Europe, in fact. From this barbaric confusion of tongues the scholar took refuge in Latin, the man of the world in French. Latin was still, as in the Middle Ages, the language of scholars all the world over; the voice of learning spoke in Latin alone. In order that the work by Martin Opitz[1] inveighing against

The German Language

---

[1] A poet and a pioneer of the literary renaissance in Germany in the early part of the century.

ENTERTAINING IN THE GARDEN

Dirck Hals

the neglect of his mother tongue should be read by those at whom it was aimed, he had to compile it in Latin. The society which met in the capacity of an official body for the study of German history issued its publications in Latin. The peace covenant finally drawn up at Münster and Osnabrück was framed in Latin. Christian Thomasius[1] was obliged to leave Leipzig University for venturing to announce that his

THE GREAT FAIR AT FLORENCE (PART)
Jacques Callot, after David Teniers the Younger. 1620

lectures would be given in German, and Moscherosch[2] once refers ironically to a scholar who had no desire to reach heaven unless Latin were spoken there. The Jesuit schools purposely treated German as a language secondary in value to Latin, the international tongue; one of the principles of the order, indeed, was to appoint only foreigners to its teaching staff. It was customary to impart instruction in Latin over a period of some fifteen or twenty years, with so little result that at the end of that time—so Comenius[3] deplores—pupils

[1] 1655–1728; the founder of German rationalism.
[2] Johann (Hans) Michael Moscherosch (1601–69), a famous German satirical novelist. His *nom de plume* was Philander von Sittewald.
[3] Johann Amos Comenius (1592–1671), a prominent educationist and the last Bishop of the Church of the Moravian and Bohemian Brethren. See p. 51.

NURSE AND CHILD
Franz Hals
*Kaiser Friedrich Museum, Berlin*

36

THE GRIMANI PLEASURE GARDENS, BETWEEN PADUA AND VENICE
Johann Wilhelm Baur

had no real knowledge of either German or Latin. The cultured man, the man of the world, naturally proceeded to despise his mother tongue as vulgar and the Latin of the scholar as pedantic; his choice of a linguistic medium lay, therefore, between Italian and French. In point of fluency and elegance of expression both these languages were superior to German; both could boast, moreover, a poetic literature

A DUTCH NOBLEMAN AND HIS WIFE
Franz Hals

of extreme beauty, endowed with a perfection of form to which German, at that time, could produce nothing comparable in attraction and charm. It was not unnatural, then, that people preferred Ariosto, Tasso, or Corneille to the Germans Lohenstein and Gryphius, and would rather read the *Clélie* or the *Artamène* of Mlle de Scudéry[1] than the *Wundergeschichte des christlichen teutschen Grossfürsten Herkules und des böhmischen königlichen Fräulein Valiska* (*The Marvellous History of his Most Christian German Royal Highness Hercules and of her Bohemian Royal Highness Lady Valiska*) whereby, in 1659, Andreas Heinrich Bucholtz[2] gladdened the hearts of the German public. A cultured German could hardly be blamed

[1] See p. 191.
[2] Andreas Heinrich Bucholtz (1607–71) and Eberhard Werner Happel (1647–90) (see p. 40) belonged to the school of writers of the 'heroic' novel of gallant adventures.

A FAMILY GROUP
Wybrand de Geest.  1621

for feeling more drawn to a rogue like Gil Blas than to Ono-gambo the Asiatic, Mandorell the Islander, Tarnolast the Africander, or Toroan the European, with whose adventures Happel[1] taxed the patience of his readers. Conscious of the lamentable state of their language and literature, Germans desirous of purifying their speech and raising the level of their literary production had no alternative but to emulate the more graceful forms and more poetic spirit of foreign works. In addition, they directly modelled the numerous philological and literary societies, such as the Palmenorden (Order of the Palm), the Pegnitzschäfer (the Pegnitz Shepherds), the Elb-Schwanen-Orden (Order of the Elbe Swan), and so on, even to their names and statutes, on the Italian academies. The services these bodies rendered to German poetic art are negligible: their real value lay in the taste they gave society for intellectual pursuits. Although the Palmenorden won no special laurels, the fact that its members included three electors, forty-nine dukes, nineteen princes, sixty counts, forty-five barons, and eighty lesser nobles was a highly creditable record for those days, and showed that even great gentlemen like these were beginning to turn to nobler pastimes than drink, gambling, and sport.

On all sides the exponents of politics, literature, and art strove to discard German for foreign standards; and so potent was the current formed by their united endeavour that it swept German culture into alien channels.

French Supremacy

That of all those foreign influences rivalling one another in Germany during the seventeenth century the French finally reigned supreme was due to the close political relations with France. Already in the sixteenth century the German Protestants had endeavoured to establish contact with the French Huguenots; Henry IV of France was greatly in sympathy with them, and even Richelieu did not refuse them his support. It was, indeed, at the courts of the Protestant German princes, at that of the Palatinate in particular,

---

[1] According to Professor J. G. Robertson (*A History of German Literature*, 1931), the chief attraction of Happel's romances was the descriptions of different parts of the globe.

that French manners were first adopted and retained; Frederick, Count Palatine, received his entire education in France. According to Count Christoph von Dohna,[1] who paid frequent visits to the court at Königsberg of Maria Eleanor of Prussia, of Rhenish descent, the Duchess preferred French to her mother tongue. Philipp Hainhofer[2] tells us that when attending the Heidelberg court in 1615 he had to

DRAWING BY HENDRICK AVERCAMP
*Print Room of the Berlin Museums*

speak French, and that French was also the language spoken at table at the court of Berlin. In his *Unvorgreifliche Gedanken* (*Unpresuming Ideas*)[3] Leibniz cavils at the preference of young people for French, but he himself wrote quite as much in French as in German. The court households of the half-French princes of Orange and of the closely related princes of Nassau and Hesse were further centres from which French conventions were spread. Thus in Germany the soil was already prepared before ever that radiant sun, Louis XIV, rose and caused the French language, French art, and French

[1] His full title was Count von und zu Dohna.
[2] German traveller, political correspondent, and art connoisseur (1578–1674).
[3] *Unvorgreifliche Gedanken betreffend die Ausübung und Verbesserung der Teutschen Sprache* (*Unpresuming Ideas concerning the Practice and Improvement of the German Language*).

41

modes to shine with such resplendence that they penetrated on all sides without difficulty. By the latter half of the seventeenth century, then, the gospel of French culture was being preached at practically all the German courts; at the court of Vienna alone Spanish etiquette still prevailed, while

at that of the Bavarian Elector-ate Italian influence continued to hold sway for some time. Sophia, Electress of Hanover, wrote in 1680 that her brother-in-law's court at Celle was to all intents and purposes French, and that Germans were no longer to be found there, which accounts for the fact that the correspondence between this lady and her brother, the Elector Charles Louis of the Palatinate, was conducted entirely in French. Upon the court at Hanover the *Mercure de France*

PORTRAIT OF A LADY
Jan Antonisz van Ravesteyn

bestowed the high praise that it conformed in every respect to the French model.

> Now France has perched so high in the tree,
> Full many lands her apes would be,

runs the rhyme of Friedrich von Logau,[1] who elsewhere commiserates with German children for not having been born straight away in France. That, without doubt, would also have stood them in better stead in Germany, where, when the choice for a post lay between a Frenchman and a German, the German was invariably passed over. The salaries obtaining at the court of Celle are a clear indication of the preference accorded to foreigners. The German Commissioner for Woods and Forests received an annual stipend of 1162 and the French Master of the Hunt one of 1587 thalers; an Italian gamekeeper got 494, a French one 421, and a German one 228 thalers. The pay of a French mule-driver was 206 thalers, while the German had to content himself with 77.

[1] Great German seventeenth-century epigrammatist.

The interests of the Imperial house were focused beyond the national frontiers—in Hungary, Italy, and Spain; and, damaging and humiliating though the invasion by Louis XIV might be, a far more formidable enemy of the Empire was the Turk, who represented throughout this century a great and constant danger. Thus, although the entire absence of

ELIZABETH, WIFE OF FREDERICK OF THE
PALATINATE ('THE WINTER KING')
Willem Jacobszoon Delff

national sentiment in Germany at this time was highly deplorable, it would be unfair to censure it too severely, since it was in the Roman Emperor of the German nation that patriotism was most conspicuously lacking. Within the kingdom every fresh Imperial election resulted in a narrowing of the Emperor's powers, so that finally he was reduced to conferring honours for love or money. He did not even share the intimacy with the electoral princes and the estates that the King of France enjoyed, and his prestige was far less. "He makes me feel sick," are the forcible words with which in 1678 Sophia, Electress of Hanover, referring to the letters of Leopold I, dares to reveal her opinion of his Imperial

43

Roman Majesty. The Emperor had little more to lose in Germany, so superficial had his relations with the Empire become. His court was in no way suited for a national centre of culture, like that of Versailles, in France. For one thing, there was a vast difference in the attitude assumed by the heads of these two courts toward the Church. Louis XIV was at heart a good Catholic; he fulfilled his religious duties with great conscientiousness—a fact which did not prevent him from emancipating himself from the influence of Rome in political matters or even from vigorously supporting the opposition of the Church in France to the Roman see. In striking contrast with the attitude of this King was the bigotry in which the Emperors of the house of Habsburg were steeped, and which reduced them to a positively doltish state of subjection to the dictates of the Church of Rome. The Emperor Ferdinand II heard Mass twice on weekdays and three times on Sundays, when he also attended two sermons and Vespers to boot. Leopold I celebrated Mass on his knees three times a day; so great was his dependence upon his Father Confessors that he used actually to submit to them the plans for his military campaigns. The Empress Eleanor walked barefoot in processions, and had her

LOUIS XIII
Unknown master

The House of Habsburg

44

The von Hutten Family
Cornelis de Vos
Alte Pinakothek, Munich

44

bracelets lined with thorns, hoping by these means to attain to heaven. What spiritual advantages could Germany possibly derive from rulers like these, whose souls remained stifled by an atmosphere of monkish superstition, who surrounded themselves with foreigners, and whose vital interests were centred abroad? The Habsburgs proclaimed their anti-German spirit from the day when they set themselves to stamp out Protestantism systematically within their national boundaries, thus barring their people from all possibility of progress.

ELIZABETH, SISTER OF LOUIS XIII
Franz Pourbus II

Not that the strictly ecclesiastical Lutheranism of the seven- **The** teenth century **Church** could be accused of making the smallest direct contribution toward the spiritual progress of mankind. But by very reason of the dogmatism that paralysed this Church, and by the way in which it left the spiritual life of its disciples to languish, it drove them out and forced them to seek new paths. Buckle ascribes the growth of national liberty in England to the fact that so weak, immoral, and despotic a man as Charles II filled the throne for a quarter of a century. Just as truly may it be said of Protestantism that its failings benefited mankind, for in the course of the seventeenth century they led men to the view that even an improvement in the state of this Church would not satisfy them and that complete emancipation from it was the only cure. It was left to the eighteenth century to carry this idea to its logical conclusion, but the seventeenth century took the initial step that paved the way.

Irreconcilable though the differences between Catholics and

MARIE DE MÉDICIS, WIDOW OF HENRY IV OF FRANCE
Franz Pourbus II. 1617

Protestants might be, still worse was the bitter hatred with which Calvinists and Lutherans pursued each other. In the intolerance and zealotry mutually displayed by these sects toward a different way of thought they were no whit better than the Papists of the Middle Ages, and whenever it lay within their power they resorted in an equally merciless manner to burning. Chancellor Crell had to pay with his life simply for upholding Calvinism; at Moscow the Lutherans drove poor scatterbrained Quirin Kuhlmann to the stake; at Stockholm they had the Stargard master tailor, Johann Bannier, beheaded for heresy. The number of Dissenters victimized by the Established Church in England between 1660 and 1680 has been estimated at some sixty thousand. This figure includes not only innumerable persons who were robbed of their property and banished, but many who were deprived of their lives. Not until 1677 did an Act of Parliament abolish the right of English bishops to have people burned simply for holding heretical views. Christian Thomasius, speaking of the narrow Pharisaism of Protestant theologians, said that Lutheranism had merely meant exchanging the wooden yoke of Popedom for an iron one. Ecclesiastical discipline was just as rigorously enforced in the Protestant as in the Catholic parts of Germany. The Saxon court was compelled to attend a sermon in church on Wednesdays, Fridays, and Sundays; at Sulzbach, so ran the court ordinance of Countess Hedwig of the Palatinate in 1636, neglect of this duty was punishable by a course of starvation.

Lutheran court preachers aspired to an influence similar to that exercised by the Father Confessors at Catholic courts; on the pretext of responsibility for the consciences of their flock they could pose as the infallible emissaries of God and poke a finger into every State and court pie. "I am not in the least curious to see the Pope," writes Sophia, Electress of Hanover, from Rome in 1664. "I have made the acquaintance of too many popes in Germany."

A GENOESE NOBLEMAN
Anthony Van Dyck

Where the clergy had acquired a measure ot secular power—in Scotland and the Huguenot provinces of France, for instance—they proved a perfect incubus. Dickson[1] may have regarded the Scottish Kirk as "the most beautifull thing under heaven," but its ministers were absolute killjoys and spread tribulation throughout the land. Feast-days were abolished, and games, pastimes, and distractions of all kinds, even such harmless pleasures as singing, dancing, and music, were proclaimed taboo. It was sinful to earn money, sinful to care for one's children, sinful—so these ministers declared— for a Christian to enjoy his food, since only the godless took

[1] David Dickson (1583(?)–1663), minister of Irvine, Professor of Divinity at Glasgow and Edinburgh, and a noted preacher.

47

pleasure in eating; it was even shameful to laugh and joke. For everything of which they deprived the people they substituted compulsory church-going. Toward 1670 the Edinburgh churches were holding thirty services a week, the sermon, of course, forming their main ingredient; the Rev. James Forbes[1] thought nothing of preaching for five or six hours on end. The communion service chained the devout for twelve hours in church, during which time patrols went round the houses, and woe betide all truants! To hold opinions contrary to those of a minister was heresy; to omit to greet him a grievous offence punishable with public penances, branding, and flogging, or with still more degrading penalties such as shaving the head on one side alone. The Church of the French Huguenots was a counterpart of the Scottish. No sooner had the Edict of Nantes guaranteed for the French Protestants the unhampered practice of their religion than their clergy too strove to gain the control over secular affairs of all kinds. According to Buckle, they were "not content to exercise their own religion, unless they could also trouble the religion of others." In 1615 the Synod of Grenoble called upon the Government to repudiate the decisions of the Council of Trent; the clergy of Béarn declared that it would be a crime

PHILIP IV OF SPAIN
Velazquez. 1623

[1] C. 1580–1634; Bishop of Edinburgh.

to permit the idolatry of the Mass. And so when Louis XIII visited Pau in 1620 he could not hear Mass in his own country.

In the churches founded by the religion of love only hatred now held sway. Well might Friedrich von Logau exclaim, "Lutheranism, Papistry, Calvinism, all three creeds exist, but where may Christianity be?" This spirit of dissension animating chiefs and spokesmen of all parties could not fail to repel and alienate those to whom belief was not so much a question of dogmatism as of conscience. As early as 1613 Brother Paolo Sarpi confided to Count Christoph von Dohna in Venice that in his opinion most of the trouble and uproar in the world was caused by the clergy with their violent tirades against heresy. In the words of Johann Arndt, "the ranting and raving" in which theologians indulged were emptying the houses of God.

PAOLINA ADORNO
Anthony Van Dyck

Believers began to sever their connexion with the official representatives of the established Churches and to seek salvation in quietude. As in England the striving of the Puritans after a more inward faith inevitably led to separation from the Established Church, the so-called Pietist movement, which Spener was thus enabled to foster, produced a further schism in the Lutheran Church. In the Catholic Church too a similar divorce was taking place among those who could not rest content with merely professing their faith but sought solace for the conscience. The storm roused in this Church by Cornelius Jansen's doctrine of Predestination stirred the minds of men in spheres far removed from that of trained dogmatists, and not only led forthwith to the production of new sects, but sent its echoes well into the succeeding century. The attitude of Jansenists to Jesuits in the Catholic Church corresponded with that of Calvinists to Lutherans in the Protestant, and while Spener was seeking a stronghold for his Christianity in the conventicles of the Pietists Molinos [1] was gathering around him in Rome sympathetic spirits who, like himself, craved inward salvation. The need for something more and better than the Church supplied was universal, and while many took refuge from the din of the militant Churches in the solitude of their chambers others, such as the Helmstedt professor Georg Calixtus and his son, endeavoured to calm the strife by reconciling Lutherans and Reformers not merely among themselves, but even with the

CHARLES I AS PRINCE OF WALES
Daniel Mytens. 1624

Catholic Church, an ideal which Leibniz also believed in and worked for. Charles Louis, Elector of the Palatinate, went so far as to build at Mannheim a concord church for Lutherans, Reformers, and Catholics.

The most beneficial result, however, of the animosity so zealously fostered by the clergy was that thinkers turned away from the narrowness of a faith founded solely on the letter

[1] Miguel de Molinos (1627–96), Spanish theologian and the chief apostle of quietism.

DAUGHTERS OF THE ARTIST
Cornelis de Vos
*Kaiser Friedrich Museum, Berlin*

of the word and embraced tolerance. "There is only one good and right religion in the world, that of honest men," declared old Colonel Webenheim to Princess Charlotte of the Palatinate, and she herself professed to think that "the Christian religions differ only in the pratings of their priests. True Christians leave all prating to the priests and superstition to the rabble, and serve God in their hearts."

Philosophy

THE LITTLE PRINCESS
Paulus Moreelse
*Photo F. Bruckmann A.-G., Munich*

MOTHER AND DAUGHTER
Anthony Van Dyck

At the same time that Chillingworth,[1] an Englishman, was urging tolerance as a duty imposed by the Protestant religion Johann Amos Comenius, of the Bohemian Brethren,[2] was advancing his educational theory of humanitarianism as a new ideal for mankind.

With their vision obscured, as it were, by some evil spell men had gone groping for many centuries along the false paths of theological speculation, blind to any understanding of reality or nature. In the seventeenth century the spell was suddenly broken, and philosophers adopted the view that doubt, not faith, was the condition of intellectual progress.

[1] William Chillingworth (1602–44), English divine and a controversialist in the cause of Protestantism.
[2] See p. 36, *n*. 3.

51

Thomas Hobbes, by postulating that the end of knowledge was not the supernatural world, but the world of phenomena, restored to the senses the rights of which faith had all too long deprived them. Then René Descartes completed the breach with a blind belief in tradition by propounding the theory

GEORGE VILLIERS, DUKE OF BUCKINGHAM
Willem J. Delff

that man should doubt everything which seemed to him uncertain, and by insisting that all "things received" should be discarded until they had been subjected to fresh examination. This newly awakened scepticism shattered the hollow nut of metaphysic. Scholastic reasoning and the tyranny of Aristotle collapsed, and philosophy joined hands with natural science to further the progress of mankind. Not until the eighteenth and nineteenth centuries was full benefit derived from the fact that thinkers had abandoned the blind alley of theology, for only then did ideas which hitherto had been the prerogative of the few become the common property of all. To the seventeenth century, however, belongs the credit for having done the spade-work by establishing natural philosophy as a recognized science. The possibility of knowing everything came to an end in the days of Kepler, Galileo, Boyle, Harvey, and Huyghens, but Newton and Leibniz made it possible instead for men to understand everything.

Germany can claim the merit of having established the first learned body of trained natural scientists; the Leopoldine Academy founded in 1652 by the Schweinfurt physician Lorenz Bausch is still extant. In 1662 the Royal Society was incorporated in London with the avowed aim of encouraging natural science in opposition to the supernatural learning which had hitherto enjoyed such monopoly, and Natural in 1666 Colbert authorized the meetings of Science the French Académie des Sciences.[1] Princes and private individuals alike interested themselves in the physical sciences.

The Emperor Rudolph called Kepler to direct his astronomical observatory in Prague; Hevelius of Danzig and Eimmart of Nuremberg possessed private observatories, the Great Elector of Brandenburg and the Grand Duke of Tuscany chemical laboratories of their own. With such zeal did the Duke of Orleans, afterward Regent, devote himself to chemical experiments that he aroused the suspicion, only too eagerly entertained at court, of following these studies solely to acquire the art of poisoning, for, as just mentioned, knowledge of

ANNE OF AUSTRIA, WIFE OF
LOUIS XIII
Peter Paul Rubens

the new sciences was at first confined to a select few, the great majority continuing in ignorance and superstition. Kepler was compelled to observe the course of the stars in order to cast horoscopes and nativities, and even leading chemical lights such as Helmont, Glauber, Becher, and others were suspected of dabbling in alchemy, which still flourished extensively. In those days alchemy was a speciality of quacks. In 1667 Friedrich Lucae met in Amsterdam a Courland nobleman in dire need, having entrusted his whole fortune of 150 ducats to an alchemist who was to transform every two of his coins into three. Similar experiences on a grander scale befell the credulous princes of Württemberg, the electors of Saxony and Brandenburg, and even the Emperor Leopold himself.

[1] The origins of the Académie are obscure.

53

A sinister belief in the powers of witches and magicians still prevailed too, and lawyers and theologians continued to **Witch** pose as the appointed representatives of ancient **Trials** prejudices. The exact number of miserable victims sent to the stake in the seventeenth century, by the theologians in the name of God and by the lawyers in the cause of human justice, is unknown, but it certainly ran into hundreds of thousands. Within a period of five years sentence was

A GENOESE LADY
Anthony Van Dyck

A DUTCH LADY
Anthony Van Dyck

passed in the principality of Neisse upon some thousand witches, including children between two and four; at Fulda the victims numbered 250 within three years, at Ellwangen 167 in a year. Between 1623 and 1631 [1] nine hundred persons of both sexes went to the stake at Würzburg; not until victims of the rack finally accused the Prince-Bishop Philipp Adolf von Ehrenberg and his councillors themselves of complicity were the eyes of the misguided authorities opened. Trials were conducted on wretchedly informal, but for the examining judge delightfully safe, lines: the accused was simply tortured until he confessed. This was an excellent way of disposing of unwelcome political opponents, as witness the deed of the Brunswickers, who accused their town-captain, the worthy

[1] Between 1627 and 1629, according to *The Cambridge Modern History*.

Henning Brabant, of being in league with the devil, and put him to death in 1604 by torture of the worst description. Never could these trials have assumed proportions so dis-

AMALIE VON SOLMS, PRINCESS OF ORANGE-NASSAU, WITH HER
SON AND DAUGHTER
Willem O. Akersloot. 1628

creditable to the name of justice had not the judges been either financially concerned in their outcome or pleasurably so in the tormenting of their victims. At Bamberg alone, for example, nine hundred witch trials resulted in the confiscation of property to the value of 500,000 gulden, and once, at Gotha, during the racking of an old woman of eighty, the judge and his assessors consumed seventeen quarts of wine and twenty-six tankards of beer. One of the chief promoters of witch trials was the Leipzig professor Benedikt Carpzow,

who, wily jurist that he was, knew how to endow every abuse of justice with the semblance of right, and in witchcraft cases deprived the accused of all legal means of defence. This most pious man, who had read the Bible from beginning to end fifty-three times, prided himself upon having affixed his signature to twenty thousand death warrants. Three Jesuits —Friedrich von Spee, Adam Tanner, and Paul Laymann—were the first persons daring enough to oppose these atrocities, and the first ruler to do so was Queen Christina

THE NUREMBERG BOOKSELLER GEORG
ENDTER AND HIS SON
Cornelius Schurtz. 1628

of Sweden, who in 1649 prohibited witch trials once and for all.

The manner in which trials of supposed magicians and witches were conducted revealed the appalling brutality of those days, a brutality equally apparent in the nature of the sentences passed on convicted criminals. Common gaol was not yet known, and the most trivial offence was punished by death or mutilation. Maritime states sent all able-bodied convicts to the galleys; in 1617 the Venetian galleys were carrying in chains two thousand men, chiefly German prisoners of war. Some rulers carried on a

Slave-
trading

PORTRAIT OF A GENTLEMAN
Unknown master
*Von Lipperheide Library of Costume, Berlin*

brisk trade in military and political prisoners. In 1674 the Emperor Leopold sold thirty-eight Lutheran clerics to Naples at fifty kronen a man. King James II of England punished the Scottish rebels by having the men's ears cut off and the women branded on cheek and brow; he then sold them as slaves to owners of plantations in Jamaica and Barbados [*sic*]. His spouse, Mary of Modena, anxious to remedy the disastrous state of her finances, participated in this profitable business. The magnanimous couple used to hand over the children of Irish captives to the court ladies so that they too might earn a little pin-money. This was how Heinrich von Üchtritz got to know the world; in 1652, with

A FRENCH GALLANT
Abraham Bosse. 1629

thirteen hundred fellow-sufferers, he was sold to the West Indies as an English prisoner-of-war, passed into the hands of

FRENCH GALLANTS
Isaac Briot II, after Jean de Saint-Igny. 1629

a Mr Whitaker in exchange for eight hundred pounds of sugar, was handed over by the latter to some Dutch merchants, and finally found himself back in his Silesian fatherland. When the provincial commander of Bilsen, who was responsible for the policing on the Lower Rhine, caught robbers he had the women and children strung up and sold the men to French bidders at ten thalers apiece. Marie de Médicis, in want of a crew for her little

57

pleasure yacht, turned to her uncle, the Grand Duke of Tuscany; the attentive uncle immediately had fifty Turks captured and presented them to his niece. Prisons, which were only destined for political offenders of the highest ranks, were kept in an appalling state. Countess Leonore Christine Ulfeldt, who, though innocent, languished for twenty-two years in the Blue Tower of Copenhagen Castle, left, in her

FRENCH GALLANTS
Abraham Bosse. 1629

*Leidensgedächtniss (Sorrowful Recollections)*, a description of her prison. The floor of the chamber which she shared with her serving-maid consisted of human excrement firmly stamped down, and the convenience, which was in the apartment, was emptied only once a week. Her tallow candle Leonore had to guard from the hungry rats, while she herself was almost eaten alive by vermin. Yet further light is shed on these times by her statement that she was visited by the Queen and the Electress of Saxony, accompanied by princesses and ladies of the court, all anxious to ascertain whether she was plagued by bugs as well as by fleas. The visit displays an astounding callousness, and it is equally distressing to find a woman of so amiable a disposition as Mme de Sévigné with nothing but irony and jeers for the innocent victims in Brittany whom the State had broken on the wheel, hanged, and quartered merely as an example to others. "Hanging seems to me a positive recreation," she wrote to the Comtesse de Grignan. If a lady of rank, a woman possessing both immense

FRENCH GALLANTS
Abraham Bosse. 1629

intellectual attraction and the highest degree of culture attainable in her day, could write like this, it is scarcely surprising if a brutalized soldiery vied with the dispensers of justice in the perpetration of barbarous and inhuman horrors.[1]

The blame for the ingrained coarseness of those days rests with the educational system, in which corporal punishment was apparently not so much the means as the end. Education Even as a crowned head Louis XIII got so much cudgelling that once he pettishly remarked that he would be better pleased with less obeisance and less whipping. Louis

[1] The author has misunderstood Mme de Sévigné's remark. What she said was, "Hanging now seems to me a deliverance"—*i.e.*, from greater miseries.

XIV fared no better; so rough was the upbringing to which the great Dauphin was subjected by the famous Bossuet that he never got over his fear of him. His tutor, the Duc de Montausier, used to drag the poor prince round the room by his hair, and he suffered equally rough treatment at the hands of the chambermaids. The future Marquise de Caylus declared herself ready to go over to the Catholic Church if only she might receive a faithful promise to be spared further cuffing. While even children of the upper classes were subjected to treatment like this, those of lesser degree were utterly defenceless against the chastisement of brutal pedagogues who quite frequently crippled their pupils. If the Jesuit system of education was onesided in that it cultivated memory and externals at the cost of independent character and judgment, at least there was one good thing about it—that the abolition of corporal punishment encouraged a sense of honour. Of all the methods devised in the seventeenth century to place education on a sounder basis than the traditional one of mere memory-training that of Comenius had the most in common with the new vision with which scientists were learning to apprehend the world. Men must be guided to achieve wisdom, said Comenius, not from books, but from contemplating the heavens and the earth; they must conduct independent study, not merely accept the observations and testimony of others. Comenius also insisted that girls must receive proper instruction, so that their knowledge should not be confined to the little they might pick up casually at home.

ENGRAVING BY ISAAC BRIOT II
After Jean de Saint-Igny. Paris, 1629

For their education was primitive in the extreme; in 1613, at the Naumburg schools, for instance, reading was all they were taught, and they only learned to write at the express wish of their parents. "Prayer-book and distaff are the fitting objects for a young girl's hand," were the words in which the great Moscherosch in 1643 addressed his daughters. Fénelon heartily endorsed this view; he considered that a knowledge of religious matters and domestic work was ample for a girl's education. In old age Mme de Maintenon was still fond of relating how in her young days her aunt would give her a piece of stale bread and a primer in which she must learn a couple of pages by heart, and then send her into the fields to mind the turkeys. Mlle de Brézé could neither read nor write when in 1641, at fourteen, she married the great Condé; she first learned these arts at the Carmelite convent at Saint-Denis, where she was placed by her husband after their marriage when he betook himself to the wars.

ENGRAVING BY ISAAC BRIOT II
After Jean de Saint-Igny. Paris, 1629

A FESTAL CHARIOT
Jacques Callot

61

## CHAPTER II
### THE ARTS

THE art of the seventeenth century, unlike that of the fifteenth and sixteenth, which followed traditional lines, was a
New
Ideals
law unto itself. It rejected the authority of classical
antiquity, to which the earlier art had bowed, and
sought new forms and methods of expression. In so doing it
was conforming to the spirit of the age, for in all spheres had

FRENCH GALLANTS
Johann Wilhelm Baur

begun a fight against tradition in which science was breaking
away from the trammels of faith and new conditions were
arising in the life of both the individual and the State. The
seventeenth century continued the struggle for the right of
individuality already in progress, and brought it to a triumphant conclusion, thus bidding a final farewell to the Middle
Ages, with their disregard of the individual. Views and
conceptions endowed by many centuries of acceptance with

incontrovertible authority collapsed, and a general transformation of ideas took place which set a totally fresh stamp
upon art, literature, learning, and society. The hostility now
experienced toward views which hitherto had been compulsory promptly expressed itself in extremes. Rule of thumb
gave way to caprice; in fact, the only rule recognized by the

ENGRAVINGS BY ISAAC BRIOT II
After Jean de Saint-Igny. Paris, 1629

new art was the law of caprice. Art acquired a character
known as 'baroque,' in the sense of something eccentric,
strange. This term, used as a mark of contempt in   Baroque
histories of art compiled during the sway of classi-   Art
cism, is no longer employed to-day in a derogatory sense, but
as characterizing not merely the art of this period, but the spirit
pervading its entire culture. For, apart from the art, literature, and mode of life of the seventeenth century, its fashions
and manner of speech became baroque. While the spirit of
the old days was natural and unstudied, that of the new,
swayed in all directions in its effort to give artistic expression
to its new-found wealth of feeling, became artificial and forced,

and conceptions ultimately grew far more extravagant than their subjects warranted. A striving in this direction was evident in all branches of the arts. Just as poets wallowed in tortured phrases, high-flown images, and forced metaphors and similes, until the little they had to express was drowned in a flood of extravagant language, so architects erected façades quite out of proportion to the size and purpose of

LOVERS
Michel Lasne

their buildings. Since from the verses themselves it was impossible to grasp the author's meaning, Claudio Achillini found it advisable to explain the gist of his poems in straightforward prose. Architects too set about their work as if they were less concerned with solving practical problems than with setting riddles. The true principle of architecture is stable equilibrium, but apparently that of seventeenth-century construction was restlessness, for walls were arched, pillars meandered, everywhere the rounded angle ousted the right angle and the curved line the straight one. Poets employed sonorous words, not because they had any sense, but for their resonance; similarly, artists revelled in meaningless forms and colours applied for mere form's or colour's sake. Art did not seek to convince by its inherent qualities, but simply to dazzle; it did not aim at entrancing the beholder, but at overwhelming him. To this end all means, including deception, were employed. Façades often rose whole storeys above the buildings that they masked, and by means of cunning perspective and subtly contrived lighting rooms were rendered altogether deceptive in proportion. Everything was staked, as in a map, on a superficial view. The artist was not concerned with creating enduring works of art, but was content to produce an overpowering first impression. Baroque art recognized no impediments or difficulties, for it mastered them in such a way that they became advantages. Thus the

THE ARTIST'S SONS
Peter Paul Rubens.  1625
*Liechtenstein Gallery, Vienna*

church of San Carlino alle Fontane, although irregular in ground-plan and poorly situated, is Borromini's most pleasing creation; with what magic, too, did Bernini conjure out of a dark, narrow passage the magnificent stairways of the Vatican.

MARIA ELEONORA OF BRANDENBURG, QUEEN OF SWEDEN
Jacob Hoefnagel. 1629

The masters of the new style—a style better adapted than any of the preceding ones to make an imposing display—the masters whose talent enabled them to turn to artistic account the need of their day for more intense expression, were Italians. Maderno, Bernini, Borromini, and Rainaldi erected their masterpieces in Rome, thereby establishing the seat of the Vicar of Christ, which ever since the latter half of the sixteenth century had represented the Nirvana of artists, as the centre of all the arts. Rome awarded the laurels of world renown; it was in Rome, too, that the masters of the Bolognese School first obtained recognition as the foremost painters of their time, a place held undisputed for many generations by Caracci, Guido Reni, Albani, and Domenichino. To be a true artist, apparently, it was essential to see Rome. Germans, Dutch, French, and Spaniards betook themselves over the Alps. Some, such as Adam Elsheimer, Nicolas Poussin, and Claude of Lorraine, could not tear themselves away from the Eternal City, while others, such as Mignard, Sandrart, and Le Brun, stayed for many decades; and not one of them escaped being very considerably influenced, not to say harmed, by the grandeur of Roman art. The sole exceptions to this rule were the three great seventeenth-century masters, Velazquez, Murillo, and Rembrandt. The former visited Rome twice without falling a victim to its charms, the other two never set foot there. Just as Rome once preached the Gospel to the North, so its emissaries now traversed the Alps to proclaim the new art to the barbarians. The works of Martinelli in Vienna, Barelli in Munich, Carlone in Passau, Solari in Salzburg, Petrini in Würzburg, and Filippo di Chiesa in Potsdam were all inspired by the great baroque masters of the South, and covered Germany with edifices reminiscent of Italy. Charles Le Brun was instrumental in introducing the style of Pietro da Cortona into France, where he applied it to the decoration of Versailles and thus assured it universal fame. Fischer von Erlach, greatest of all the German exponents of baroque, gave Vienna its attractive character by the masterly way in which he adapted the elaborate style of Italian art to the majestic requirements of an Imperial court.

Spaciousness and sumptuous decoration—the advantages of the baroque style—were most suited to ecclesiastical and **Domestic** palace architecture, but even in the latter they **Archi-** remained superficial advantages, for they were **tecture** better adapted to display than comfort. In Germany domestic architecture never partook of this style, nor was it applied to castles there until nearly the end of the century. Riedinger's magnificent castle at Aschaffenburg, the

CARICATURE OF GERMAN FASHIONS

1629

last of the great palaces erected before the Thirty Years War, which towers, a mass of glowing colour, over the Main, is pure Renaissance in character. It combines the typical ground-plan of a fortified castle finished at the four corners with towers with an interior retaining all the discomforts of the Middle Ages; its narrow, winding stairs and awkwardly connected rooms still bear witness to early ideas of planning. In places such as the royal residence at Bamberg and the castle of Rosenborg in Copenhagen the great banqueting hall is also poked away on an upper floor and lacks a direct approach. A similar state of affairs existed in France, where even the court was slow to emulate the far more advanced style of Italian architecture. When Marie de Médicis took up residence at the Louvre great was her dismay at its shabby, uncomfortable aspect, and she thought that either it was not the King's residence or she was the victim of a practical joke. Yet France also clung obstinately for many decades to the traditional system of ground-planning. Except for the fact that pavilions had taken the place of corner towers, the castle of Versailles, erected by Louis XIII in 1624, and that rebuilt by Cardinal Richelieu in Poitou retained the character of forts. Even when Marie de Médicis expressed the wish for a palace executed in the Italian manner, Salomon de Brosse drafted designs for the Luxembourg which were definitely French in style. When Louis XIV proposed to improve the Louvre Colbert, losing his temper over the plans submitted

AMALIE VON SOLMS, PRINCESS OF
ORANGE-NASSAU
Willem J. Delff. 1629

by French architects, sent word of the project to Rome and invited the competition of such famous Roman masters as Rainaldi and Bernini. But although Bernini is known to have journeyed to Paris to compete, the Frenchman Perrault triumphed. The façade of the Louvre was executed in accordance with his plans, and French classicism carried the day against Roman baroque. But old-style architecture had now ceased to find general favour; Venturini denounced the Alcazar of the Spanish kings in Madrid as cheerless and dark, and declared that it contained

HÉLÈNE FOURMENT
Peter Paul Rubens. 1630

not a single good room. The archducal residence at Innsbruck struck Hainhofer in 1628 as "old-fashioned and melancholy," and Misson in 1687 found Heidelberg Castle "melancholy and unpleasing." Charlotte of the Palatinate, however, with her touching love of the Fatherland, said of Fontainebleau, "What pleases me about this place is that all the galleries and rooms look German." In reality Fontainebleau owed this appearance to Italian artists of the sixteenth century, and the 'German' elements in the French castle which this Duchess of Orleans found so pleasing were the Renaissance decoration and planning of the rooms common to all old-fashioned castles in those days.

BARON KINSKI
Lucas Kilian. 1630

Italian artists of the seventeenth century concentrated their attention upon making halls, staircases, and state rooms spacious and ornate, and left the comfort of the inmates to look after itself. Their French contemporaries were the first

CLAUDE DERUET AND HIS SON
Jacques Callot. 1632

to pay any heed to this side of the question. In the castle of Vaux-le-Vicomte, near Melun, built by Levau for Fouquet, and the Hôtel de la Vrillière, in Paris, erected by Mansart, interior planning took account for the first time of such things as the provision of separate entrances and passage-ways for the staff, thus furnishing the earliest indications of a new stage of culture with new requirements and demands. Not until the eighteenth century was the principle to be further developed and adopted in Germany. The Royal Palace in Berlin, rebuilt[1] by Schlüter, did not contain any of these improvements; its rooms still led one into the other, and there were no service passages to lighten the work of the staff. In Germany middle-class residences equipped with any degree of comfort must have been very rare; at all events, the house of Professor Weigel at Jena passed on this account for many decades as one of the sights of the country. There are houses of this date still standing at Nuremberg, Munich, and other

[1] Between 1699 and 1706.

70

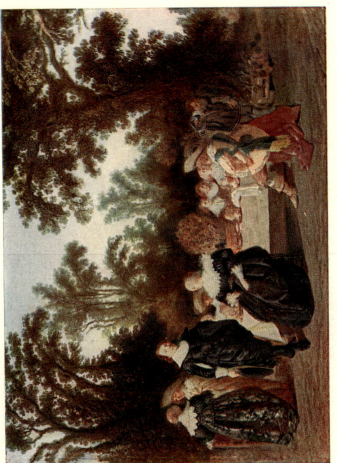

A Garden Party
Anthonie Palamedesz
*Kaiser Friedrich Museum, Berlin*

old towns, which show how modest were the claims made then in respect of ventilation, light, and general comfort. As in the typical example of the Peller house,[1] erected in 1605, the front rooms are large and lofty—often too large—the staircase is dark, the back rooms are windowless and depend for light and air upon the open gallery along which they run.

Lighting must have been rendered additionally unsatisfactory by the fact that the window-panes seldom consisted of clear glass. The much-travelled Philipp Hainhofer was astounded to see in 1611 at the castle of Wilibald, near Eichstätt, "fine light windows with great transparent panes, through which one might easily put one's head." Glass windows remained for many years to come a great luxury; the poor people could not always afford even bull's-eye glass, and had to content

JACQUES CALLOT THE ENGRAVER
Lucas Vorsterman, after Van Dyck

themselves with stretching paper across their windows. In the south windows all consisted of paper; bitter were the complaints of travellers like Misson that frames covered with paper or linen (*impannate*) did not keep out the cold.

The general character of the German towns testified to this slow development in comfort; their recovery from the ravages of the great war was very slow. Adam Samuel Urban Hartmann, who made a tour of Germany in 1657– Conditions 59, found Angermünde "a deserted, miserable little town, with scarcely a house entire," and Lucae, ten years later, passed on his journey through the Mark "semi-deserted

[1] A well-known house at Nuremberg, built in the Venetian style.

71

townships, inhabited by a wretched collection of grotesque and hideous folk." "Elsewhere six such towns would scarcely have composed a village," was his further comment. In 1687 Misson calls Nuremberg "a fine town," but promptly qualifies this praise by saying, "although there is something Gothic

SIR JOHN ELIOT
Painted in the Tower of London. 1632

and old-fashioned about the buildings, the architecture of which is not of the best." Only in princely residences and coastal towns was any progress made. In 1671 Chappuzeau describes Stuttgart as a beautiful city, and is absolutely enchanted with Dresden. Plain-spoken Pastor Hartmann finds the buildings in Berlin and Cologne "clean, and for the most part handsome"; "even at Breslau they are no finer," hastens to add this loyal Silesian. His verdict on Hamburg, that he has seldom seen "a more magnificent city," is followed by the remark, "but its streets and alleys are very narrow, dirty, and dark." The Italian towns, with their high level of artistic culture, remained head and shoulders above the rest. Sophia, Electress of Hanover, delighted though she was with what met her eyes at Verona, Vicenza, Bologna, and other Italian places, on arriving in Rome, which boasts some of the most beautiful houses and gardens in the world, thought she had been wafted to paradise. Misson, whose travels succeeded those of the German princess by over twenty years, proved far more exacting. While she, equally with us to-day, was greatly impressed by the palaces of Vicenza, and by the Rotonda[1] in particular, he dismisses them with the disdainful remark that the Italians have a habit of dubbing every massive structure a *palazzo*, and that the term is applied in a far less wholesale manner in England. During the latter half

A RED VELVET COAT OF COUNT TILLY
1632
*National Museum of Bavaria, Munich*

of the seventeenth century originated the idea of laying out whole towns or quarters artistically on a systematic plan, an innovation in which Italy again took the lead. After the Great Fire of London designs for reconstruction were prepared by Sir Christopher Wren.[2] The Palais-Royal in Paris

[1] A villa designed by Palladio, a famous Italian architect of the sixteenth century.

[2] Apart from St Paul's and the other City churches restored according to his design, Wren also prepared a scheme for laying out the whole of the City on a new plan, but it was abandoned owing to complications connected with the ownership of the land.

and its side-streets were begun in the reign of Louis XIII. "Indescribably beautiful" were the words applied to this quarter, with its strictly regular planning, by the enraptured Pastor Hartmann. But the street litter in those days must have been truly appalling; London, in particular, had the name of being one of the dirtiest cities, and as most of the townsfolk in impoverished Germany went in for farming

THE ANATOMY LESSON OF PROFESSOR TULP (PART)
Rembrandt. 1632
*Photo F. Bruckmann A.-G., Munich*

the state of affairs was no better in the towns there. From 1671 every peasant coming to market with a cart in Berlin was bound to remove a cartload of refuse, and in 1681 the Great Elector forbade the inhabitants of Berlin to keep pigs because the stys were blocking and fouling the streets. Conditions were equally bad everywhere in regard to street lighting, which was introduced in Paris in 1667, in London in 1668, and in Amsterdam in 1669. Berlin followed suit in 1679, Vienna only in 1687, Hanover in 1696. As even large towns still favoured timbered buildings with shingle and thatched roofs there was constant risk of fire. A great number of bad fires were, in fact, recorded in the seventeenth century; Passau was burned down three times, and the Great Fire of 1666 in

London destroyed eighty-nine churches [1] and some thirteen thousand houses. Fire-engines were first used in Germany: Bremen had them in 1656, Nuremberg two years later; they were introduced in Paris in 1669, but in London not until 1688.

If the organization of public welfare and the state of domestic comfort left practically everything to be desired, making life, according to present-day standards, **Furniture** uncomfortable, not to say rough, people were equally unspoiled in regard to furniture. Articles of furniture were remarkably limited, and included, in the early days, neither settee, wardrobe, chest of drawers, nor writing-table. Clothing and linen were kept in chests; upon the arrest of the wife of Marshal d'Ancre twenty chests containing her wardrobe were seized. The settee proper only developed toward the end of the century [2]—not, strange to say, from the bench, but the bed. Throughout the century ladies used to receive their callers in bed or seated thereon; an invitation to share this seat was considered a great honour. The Duke de Olivares, Minister to Philip IV, even gave audience to ambassadors in bed. Great attention was therefore bestowed on bed furnishings. Just before the Saxon Chancellor, von Beichling, was removed to the Königstein [3] he had purchased a new set of green moire bed hangings worth 2500 thalers. Among the designs executed by Daniel Marot, Le Pautre, and other artists in furniture and interior decoration the bed played a prominent part. In these designs may be traced the gradual development, from the bed, of a couch somewhat resembling the present-day ottoman; finally, some ingenious brain, not content with giving this couch supports at the ends, joined these supports along one side by means of upholstery, and so produced the settee. The chest of drawers (*commode*) also delayed its appearance until the turn of the seventeenth and eighteenth centuries, [4] and the writing-table until the

---

[1] W. G. Bell, in *The Great Fire of London*, gives the figure as eighty-seven.
[2] But *cf.* the Stuart 'day-bed.'
[3] A fortress in Saxony.
[4] The earliest form of English chest of drawers—the oak chest with two drawers beneath—occurs in the Cromwellian period.

eighteenth.[1]  Not only was furniture very limited in kind, but even people of position owned quite small stocks.  When the French court invited foreign ambassadors to Fontainebleau

GUSTAVUS ADOLPHUS OF SWEDEN
Willem J. Delff

the latter were requested to bring their own beds, hangings, and crockery.  Once, when Marie de Médicis was expecting a visit from her sister Eleanor, Duchess of Mantua, she begged her court banker, de Gondi, who owned the finest and most elegant palace in Paris, to offer hospitality to the duchess.

[1] Writing bureaux, especially copies of Dutch patterns based on the Parisian bureaux, existed in Germany in 1690.

TWO UNKNOWN LADIES OF RANK
Miniatures
*National Museum of Bavaria, Munich*

76

This he agreed to do on receipt of the necessary furniture; so the Queen, being unable to supply it, wrote and begged some on loan from all her acquaintances. If grand houses owned but little furniture this little was, at any rate, distinguished by its sumptuous style. A favourite article in the early part of the century was the cabinet. Known as a writing-desk, it did not correspond with this object in the present-day sense; rather was it, as Schlosser says, a veritable microcosm, presenting in make, decoration, and content a whole cyclopædia of the physical and moral world. The most famous example is probably the Pomeranian cabinet, now housed in the Berlin Museum of Art and Industry. Intended not for use, but as a toy, it contains, apart from writing materials, implements of all kinds—drinking vessels, articles of toilet, including a brush and comb, plates, glasses,

A GOLD-EMBROIDERED VIOLET SILK SUIT
OF GUSTAVUS ADOLPHUS OF SWEDEN
*Royal Armoury, Stockholm*

instruments, games, even a minting machine, the objects being concealed one within the other in the most ingenious way. The literary ornamentation of these cabinets, with its classical allusions and profound allegories, bore on a definite period, and the divining of them was intended as food for the owner's wits. These marvels of technical skill cost a small fortune; the Duke of Stettin gave over 20,000 gulden in 1617 for the Pomeranian cabinet. Philipp Hainhofer had several magnificent pieces of this kind made at Augsburg after his own designs. One of these the town council purchased in 1632 for 9750 gulden and presented to Gustavus Adolphus; it now belongs to the Upsala Library. Another, worth 6000 gulden, Hainhofer conveyed in person to Innsbruck in 1628. In 1611 the Bishop of Eichstätt owned three costly cabinets of this nature, one of which alone had cost him 14,000 gulden. A writing-desk, now the property of the Saxon Art Collection, executed at Dresden by Hans Schifferstein in 1615 for 3000 gulden, contains 120 drawers, and the wonderful

THE LACE COLLAR OF GUSTAVUS ADOLPHUS OF SWEDEN
WORN AT AUGSBURG IN 1632

ivory coin-cabinet made by Christoph Angermeier for Duke Maximilian of Bavaria is now one of the chief treasures of the National Museum of Bavaria.

In pursuance of medieval practice tapestries were still employed as wall decorations; so widespread, indeed, did the taste for this fine style of furnishing become in the course of the century that rulers all installed *haute-lisse* [1] works in their capitals. Velazquez has painted a picture of the workshop in the Madrid factory. Workshops of this kind sprang up throughout Germany—in Berlin, Dresden, Munich, and Vienna—and sought to rival the famous products of the French Gobelin industry. When persons of princely rank went travelling they took their tapestries with them. The wooden pavilion erected to harbour the French and Spanish courts which forgathered in

*Tapestries*

---

[1] A tapestry hanging made on an upright loom, in contrast to *basse-lisse* tapestry, made on a horizontal one.

1660 in the Island of Pheasants on the Bidassoa river was rendered positively palatial by the hangings brought with them by the respective monarchs, the decoration of the Spanish portion of the pavilion being entrusted to Velazquez. In 1687 Misson valued the tapestry stocks of the Munich court at eight million thalers. Middle-class folk, who could not afford such luxuries, continued to line their walls with wainscoting or resorted to linen, and wallpapers now made their first appearance. In 1634 a certain Jerome Lanyer in England obtained a licence for the manufacture of wallpapers, and in 1688 a similar licence was granted by Louis XIV to Papillon, the wood-engraver. At first wallpapers met with scant approval in better-class homes, for the moneyed classes were beginning to evince a taste for pictures. The manner

PORTRAIT OF A MERCHANT
Thomas de Keyser

in which the seventeenth century learned to appraise and cultivate art revealed an entirely new sense of values. In the early days real connoisseurs were very rare—even people of great wealth and culture had always Collectors delighted far more in curios than in genuine works of art. The collections of art and curios in royal and private hands contained everything imaginable in the shape of natural and artistic objects. Stuffed animals, fossils, turnery products, and all kinds of knick-knacks were housed alongside pictures by first-class masters, classical statuary, bronzes, and the like. The national art collections in Berlin, Brunswick, Dresden,

79

Cassel, Gottorp, and elsewhere were of this nature. The diaries and travel books of Philipp Hainhofer, wherein this Augsburg art patron, collector, and dealer has so graphically recorded his travels to Dresden, Stettin, Heidelberg, and Innsbruck, afford an excellent guide to the higgledy-piggledy collection of objects which fell within the province of dealers in those days, and to the manner in which these dealers effected their bargains and exchanges. Mere curios and bizarreries were just as highly prized then as real works of art. Even Hainhofer, who passed for an authority in such matters and for a great connoisseur, sometimes gave voice to pictorial criticisms which place his artistic judgment in a very dubious light. During the course of the seventeenth century, however, this whole class of collectors was gradually supplanted by true connoisseurs and finally disappeared. The Emperor Rudolph II, the most illustrious and at the same time—judging by the extent of his collections—most zealous collector of his day, was undoubtedly a survivor of the old school; the medley of objects which he assembled at the Hradschin [1] was still a jumble of the most heterogeneous nature. It is true that in his gallery of some eight hundred pictures he possessed originals by Raphael, Titian, Correggio, Dürer, Holbein, and other first-class masters, but they were just stacked up, one on top of the other, and after his death both they and the antiques were found in the neglected state in which they had been left for years. The crowned heads of that time, however, could boast in Philip II a true connoisseur who conducted his patronage of art on genuinely æsthetic lines. He passed on this gift to his grandson, Philip IV, the owner of one of the finest art galleries of his day. He was lucky, of course, in having Velazquez at his disposal both as adviser and as enricher of his collection, for this artist served no other sovereign in the same way. His rivals were Charles I of England, supported by Van Dyck, and the Archduke Leopold William, with David Teniers the Younger. The aforesaid Spanish and Austrian art collections rank among the finest in modern eyes; the Prado and the State galleries

---

[1] Or Hradčany Palace, the former royal residence in Prague.

in Vienna, where they are lodged, owe their most valuable acquisitions to the cultured taste of these illustrious rulers. Italians had for many years regarded the possession of art treasures as essential to *bon ton*; the nepotic families of the Borghese, Barberini, Aldobrandini, and other Popes, made this their first concern. The great lords north of the Alps and

beyond the seas now became fired by their example, and Spanish, French, and English aristocrats contrived to amass some priceless treasures. The Earl of Arundel[1] was the first to send expeditions to Greece to carry on private excavations. The founding of large galleries, entirely dependent upon Italy as the source of supply, naturally led to a wholesale production of fakes. As the ambition of every collector was to own pictures by great masters, works by Titian, Giorgione, Palma, and others were eagerly sought, and, expert criticism being still

THE COMTE D'HARCOURT,
"CADET LA PERLE"
Jean Morin

in its infancy, Italian dealers supplied by the score enough originals to meet the demand.

Love of art remained by no means confined, however, to courts and great patrons, and the fostering it received during this century at the hands of the middle classes possibly aided the cause of art, as such, more effec- **Painting** tively than did the united patronage of all the courts. The awakening of individuality, which was such a conspicuous feature of the seventeenth century, causing men to become conscious of and rejoice in their egos, greatly benefited painting in that it promoted the art of portraiture. There is nothing fortuitous in the fact that the seventeenth century was the century of great portraitists. If all the pictures painted

[1] Thomas Howard, second Earl of Arundel (*c.* 1585–1646).

between 1600 and 1700 were assembled a glance would show the great part played by portraiture in this period and the way in which it usurped the place of the religious subject picture which had for so long constituted the chief ingredient of artistic output. The School of Bologna, the beginnings of which date back to the middle of the sixteenth century, was almost devoid of portraits proper, the Caracci and their pupils painted scarcely any, and the innumerable idealistic heads by Guido Reni do not bear the stamp of portraits. In the seventeenth century the position became practically reversed. Throughout the works of the great masters of this period portraiture struck the dominant note, for no sooner was there a call for this type of work than it met with a magnificent response. Velazquez, the greatest of these masters, "le plus peintre qui ait jamais existé" ("the painter of painters"),[1] produced little but portraits. When Philip IV had once got hold of Velazquez he refused to part with him, and served him as a model for many years. That this pitiable monarch and his absurdly dreary court have not faded into oblivion they owe solely to the brush of their court painter, which endowed them with a share of immortality. Every ruler of this century kept his court painter busy with a succession of portraits. Rubens executed any number of the Infanta Isabella Clara Eugenia, Sustermanns of the Medicis, Mignard and Rigaud of Louis XIV. Van Dyck painted Charles I forty and Queen Henrietta Maria thirty times, produced nine portraits of the Earl of Strafford, seven of the Earl of Arundel, and four in a year of Lady Digby. A regular portrait mania! After this recital of the triumphs of vanity it is truly refreshing to glean from the lips of Sophia of the Palatinate[2] a naïve confession of the false impression she derived from Van Dyck's portraits. Before she became personally acquainted with Queen Henrietta Maria and her ladies-in-waiting she had expected to meet exquisite beauties. What was her bitter disappointment to find that this beautiful Queen had crooked shoulders, long, lean arms, and prominent teeth!

---

[1] W. Bürger (E. J. T. Thoré, a French exile and eminent art critic), *Velazquez et ses œuvres* (1865), p. 235.      [2] See p. 91, *n.* 2.

THE MARQUIS DE MIRABELLA
Anthony Van Dyck
*Alte Pinakothek, Munich*                    82

Throughout the century portraiture remained an art popular among all classes of society. Those who could not afford to be painted had their likenesses engraved on copper. Nuremberg and Augsburg were the homes of scores of skilled engravers whose sole occupation was the portrayal of patricians, burghers, and craftsmen. Just as ladies a couple of

THE DRESS OF A FRENCH COURTIER AFTER THE EDICT OF 1633
Abraham Bosse

hundred years later were induced by the facility of photography to pose to the camera in every new hat, so people of means in those days were nothing loth to sit for their portraits —a new coiffure or lace collar provided reason enough; and one can often see where the engraver has made alterations in a plate in order to bring an old-fashioned cut of hair and beard up to date. The whole character of the time, its gradual progress from the simple to the theatrical, is revealed in these seventeenth-century portraits. How restful and dignified do the conceptions of Philippe de Champaigne even now appear in comparison with Rigaud's sitters, striving, with their look of proud pathos, to be numbered among the great; and if Van Dyck's canvases mirror the affected mannerisms of a generation which modelled its behaviour on the pastoral poems of Marini and d'Urfé, the spirit behind Kneller's portraits —his beauty gallery at Hampton Court ranks foremost of its kind—frankly breathes equality with the gods.

THE DRESS OF A FRENCH COURTIER AFTER
THE EDICT OF 1633
Abraham Bosse

Very different from the products of these court painters and their circles is the art with which the citizens of Holland have endowed—nay, blessed—mankind! While the former seek only to impose, and all the sitters, even the King, seem anxious to appear greater than they are, the Dutch burgher presents a simple, unpretentious front. So alive, so imbued with a character of wholesome, almost matter-of-course honesty, are the portraits by Jordaens, Cornelis de Vos, van der Helst, and others—let alone Rembrandt and Franz Hals—

that even the simplest among them bear the stamp of genius.
It was this homely character of the Dutch, this quality of
naturalness distinguishing painter and sitter alike, which produced the *genre* picture. The appeal both of home and
outdoor surroundings opened the eyes of Dutch painters to
the artistic possibilities of interiors, of the play of light and
shade in enclosed spaces, of the delightful vistas along their
streets and canals. They immortalized not only the elusive

PORTRAIT OF A YOUNG MAN
Franz Hals

sun-ray darting through a chink in the wall, but light stream-
ing full flood between wide-flung casements. Their studies
ranged from the burgher tarrying in his quiet chamber to
the noisy bustle of the fair; they reproduced equally well
the uproarious humour of the tipsy peasant and the prim
dignity of the well-born councillor. David Teniers, Gerard
Dou, Gabriel Metsu, Franz Mieris, Ter Borch, Vermeer, and
Jan Steen, to name but a few, were keenly alive to the vigorous
pulsating of Dutch life, and whereas in the seventeenth century Holland was practically the only European state to offer
a haven of peace amid the din of war, so the Dutch art of this
century also differed radically from that of the other European

lands. The Dutch, who learned to gaze around them in such unaffected joy, were likewise the first to feel that devotion to nature which was to imbue landscape painting with a totally new spirit. Ruisdael and Meindert Hobbema, among others, discovered in atmospheric effect a fascination which no one had so far realized. Allart van Everdingen,[1] travelling in Norway for purposes of study, was the first to experience no

AN OPEN-AIR PARTY
In the background are Heidelberg Castle and its grounds.
Jacques Fouquier

feeling of terror in the great mountain fastnesses; where others had seen only haunted solitudes what impressed him was the magnificence of rock and crag.

It was inevitable that in the endeavour to give stronger expression to the intensified feelings of the age the seventeenth century should turn to the stage. In architecture light and shade were now being taken into account to produce effects to an extent which proclaimed a new principle. Still more evident was this in the welding of the arts which ensued in this period. Such was the harmony

The Stage

[1] A Dutch engraver, 1620–75.

between architecture, sculpture, and painting evolved in the masterpieces of the century that perfect unity was achieved. Those of Bernini's works which he, no less than his contemporaries, considered his best are not the creation of one art alone, but of all the arts combined. The group of St Theresa with the angel, who is trying to pierce the saint with the dart of divine love, is a monument which cannot be detached from its surroundings, neither from the invisible source of light which illumines it nor from the composition in coloured marble supporting it. The architectural structure of the cathedra in St Peter's blends in a similar manner with the figures modelled in the round, with the stained-glass window to which it leads up, and with the gold and silver beams that radiate from it, to produce an effect of unity. Even the waters of the great fountain in the Piazza Navona assist toward achieving the whole conceived by the artist. This

DRAWING BY ANTHONIE PALAMEDESZ
*Print Room of the Berlin Museums*

assiduous use of every means to an end, this striving after effect, which induced Bernini, in his great architectural masterpieces —the colonnades of St Peter's, the Scala Regia, and the church at Ariccia—to rely upon optical delusion, show to what an extent the laws governing stagecraft were influencing artists in other spheres. It goes without saying that stage practice, based as it is entirely upon illusory effect, derived immense advantage from this principle. During the seventeenth century dramatic art did, indeed, attain so high a degree of perfection that nothing remained for subsequent generations but to introduce new methods of technique ; no fundamental changes were required. It was only natural that Bernini, the chief master of baroque, should place his art at the service of the theatre. He is said to have originated the idea of heightening stage effect by bringing on as accessories persons

A FLEMISH NOBLEMAN
François Duchatel

having no actual part in the play, and to have created some truly remarkable schemes of stage decoration. He once produced with such reality a scene representing the Tiber furiously bursting its banks that the audience sprang up in panic; on another occasion he obtained a similar result by his realistic staging of a conflagration.

Interest at this time was focused on the theatre, and here it is impossible to distinguish cause and effect, for technical advance in stagecraft went hand in hand with the rise of great playwrights and the progress of dramatic art, and the seventeenth century, which witnessed the formation of the first regular theatrical companies, was the era of Shakespeare, Calderon, Lope de Vega, Corneille, Racine, and Molière. In Germany Henry Julius, Duke of Brunswick, maintained his own troupe of professional players, and wrote plays for them himself. The call for theatres may be gauged from the fact that the first permanent structures for this purpose were erected in Germany while the Thirty Years War was still devastating the country. Nuremberg built its first theatre in 1628, Hanover in 1636, Ulm in 1641; next came Munich, to be followed by Dresden in 1664 with a house that could accommodate two thousand spectators. During the early part of the century some English comedians came from the Low Countries to Germany. Their productions apparently left much to be desired as regards morality. So crude were their performances, and in such vulgar obscenities did they indulge, that it was hardly surprising if the Puritans, with their strict morality, when they came into power in England immediately had all the theatres closed. These English comedians were succeeded by German strolling players; Johann Velten's company enjoyed considerable notoriety in the latter part of the century, and constituted in Dresden, where they were installed from 1685 to 1692, the first German court theatre. Their manager had translated Molière's comedies, and

CORNELIS DE GRAEF, BURGOMASTER OF AMSTERDAM
Nicolaes Eliasz

produced them on a German stage for the first time during the carnival at Torgau in 1690. Morality plays, such as the ancient *Everyman*, were also given. The Emperor Ferdinand II had a taste for tales of the martyrs, but even in these times plenty of true tragedies were set before the public. Gryphius lost no time in presenting his *Ermordete Majestät, oder Carolus Stuardus* (*The Murder of His Majesty, or Charles Stuart*); August

Adolf von Haugwitz dramatized the story of Wallenstein's murder, and Christian Weise the history of Masaniello.[1] Nor did the stage lack a political element, for in 1613 Count Christoph von Dohna saw in Berlin *Der ungerechte Haushalter*

CATARINA HOEFT, WIFE OF CORNELIS DE GRAEF
Nicolaes Eliasz

(*The Unjust Steward*), a play clearly aimed at the Elector of Brandenburg, and in Vienna the Empress Claudia Felicitas had played before the Emperor Leopold the *Lanterna di Diogene* (*The Lantern of Diogenes*), a piece in which the whole court was vilified and the Emperor confronted with a picture of his own amiable weaknesses. Henry IV of France used to derive the greatest amusement from hearing himself abused on the stage in connexion with the high rates of taxation. As German productions either abounded in horrors or were utterly insipid more cultured folk preferred French ones. In 1679 Charles Louis, Elector of the Palatinate, expressed keen disappointment with the German players and decided to engage a French company, whom he paid at the rate of forty thalers a play. Ever since 1669 the Dukes of Hanover had jointly maintained a French troupe of twenty-four persons who played for four-monthly periods at Celle, Hanover, and

[1] An Amalfi fisherman who led the revolt against Spanish rule in Naples in 1647 and was later murdered by the populace.

QUEEN MARIA ANNA OF HUNGARY
Velazquez.   1630
*Kaiser Friedrich Museum, Berlin*                    90

Osnabrück in turn. The theatre was regarded as a valuable aid to education. The Jesuits showed great zeal in producing Latin school dramas, and spent large sums in staging them. Lohenstein had his blood-and-thunder dramas played by the pupils of St Magdalen and St Elizabeth at Breslau, Christian Weise his tragedies by those of the Zittau Gymnasium. Mme de Maintenon established at Saint-Cyr[1] a theatre for which

BURGOMASTER BAS JACOBSZ AND HIS FAMILY
Dirck van Santvoort

Racine wrote the plays. But she soon saw that the girls were entering too wholeheartedly into their parts, and the young lady destined to become the Marquise de Caylus, having played her part too well, was not permitted to act again. Sophia of the Palatinate,[2] when only eleven, appeared with her sisters in Corneille's *Médée*. Theatricals were a form of entertainment which naturally found favour in all places and among all classes. Even in Rome Bernini and his pupils would lay aside their professional work during carnival time and give themselves heart and soul to play-acting. While Bernini was appearing in pieces of his own composition Salvator Rosa was neglecting his painting to wander about with a theatrical car, and was playing in improvised comedy

---

[1] Where she had founded a convent for the education of daughters of the nobility.

[2] Daughter of Frederick of the Palatinate ('the Winter King') (see p. 107, *n.* 2), afterward Electress of Hanover, the mother of our King George I.

under the name of Signor Formica. Even nuns were seized
by stage fever; at the time of Pope Innocent XI such a dispute arose in a Roman convent over the casting of parts in
a play selected for performance by its pious inmates that these

THE DRESS OF A LADY OF THE FRENCH COURT AFTER
THE EDICT OF 1633
Abraham Bosse

brides of Christ came to blows and one of them was killed.
For courts, bound as they were by the rules of an iron etiquette, if human relations were to be maintained between
ruler and subjects, theatricals were a real necessity. A kind
of mummery, called a *Wirtschaft*,[1] was therefore devised at

[1] Literally, 'inn-keeping.'

which, for the duration of the festival, the ruling prince and princess took the parts of host and hostess, the court those of serving-men and maids, house-boys, and so on. Germans were particularly fond of this kind of diversion, and frequent mention of such *Wirtschaften* occurs in the letters of Sophia, Electress of Hanover, for they provided a very useful means of solving the endless difficulties created by points of etiquette when guests of note had to be entertained. At the most formal of the European courts— that of Vienna—*Wirtschaften* be-came, indeed, quite a regular in-stitution, and recourse was always

AN UNKNOWN LADY
Paulus Moreelse

had to them when difficulties of ceremonial arose in the reception of distinguished guests. In 1698, for instance, the

A DUTCH GALLANT
Pieter Nolpe, after Peeter Quast

only way in which the Emperor Leopold and Peter the Great could meet was at a *Wirtschaft*. They performed with great gusto their respective parts as host and peasant guest, toasting one another in the manner customary on such occasions until a fairly recent date.

Out of these great court festi-vals arose, in the course of the seventeenth century, the opera. Tournaments had come to an end in the six-teenth century, their place being taken by tilting at the ring on horseback, a sport which in its turn made way for the equestrian ballet

Opera

in allegorical guise. Festivities lasted for several days, and were conducted according to a fixed programme which always partook of an allegorical and mythical character, featuring triumphs of virtue or of love, mythical marriages, or the Golden Age. A gala on the Arno in 1608 represented the expedition of the Argonauts to fetch the Golden Fleece, and when Charles II (the Impotent) of Spain wedded the poor Princess of Orleans the celebrations in Paris pictured the fall of the Kingdom of the Amazons. Count Bentivoglio was responsible for the idea underlying the great equestrian *fête*

A MERRY PARTY
Pieter Codde

organized in 1634 by Cardinal Antonio Barberini in honour of Prince Alexander Charles Vasa in the Piazza Navona, in Rome; the Princesses Anna Colonna and Constance Barberini acted as patronesses, and the whole of the Roman nobility participated. The idea for the famous festival of the enchanted island attended by Louis XIV at Versailles in 1664 was taken from Ariosto, and represented the incident of Orlando on the island of Queen Alcina. The marriage of the ·Emperor Leopold with the Infanta Margaret Theresa of Spain was celebrated at Vienna in 1667 with a spectacle figuring Paris awarding the apple to the fairest of the Graces —who was, of course, the Imperial bride. The preparations occupied nine months, Italians devised the scenario and stage machinery and composed the music, and the whole of the Austrian nobility—the families of Lobkowitz, Dietrichstein, Colloredo, Starhemberg, and Waldstein—headed by the Emperor himself, took part. Festivities of this nature resolved themselves into a procession of nymphs, fauns, shepherds,

MAKING MUSIC
Michiel Limborch

knights, Indians, and furies, and a round of equestrian quadrilles, ballets, pyrotechnical displays, serenades, theatricals, and so on. The costumes were, of course, magnificent in the extreme, and their cost correspondingly lavish. The tourney and tilt held at the Louvre court in 1662 cost 1,200,000 francs; in the Viennese equestrian ballet of the *Pomo d'Oro* (*Golden Apple*) each of the forty horses wore trappings costing 100 gulden and plumes worth 100 ducats; the producer was raised by the Emperor to baronial rank, and presented with a gift of 20,000 gulden and an annual pension of 1000 gulden.

The *pièces de résistance* of these miscellanies of costume, dance, and song were the stage machines. Not only did the actual stage-settings comprise the most ingenious and fantastical contrivances, but there were also mechanical devices which picked up the performers and swung them through the air

A YOUNG COUPLE
Pieter Codde. 1634
*Photo F. Bruckmann A.-G., Munich*

or propelled them underground. So important a part did these stage mechanisms play that Corneille, in 1650, in the "Foreword" to his *Andromède*, acknowledged them to be the essential part of the play, whereby the plot was held together and unravelled. The paraphernalia for these entertainments supplied the whole of the stage-setting necessary to opera, and since music had developed in a similar direction, here at last was real opera! Toward the end of the sixteenth century

PHILIP, LORD WHARTON, AS A SHEPHERD
Anthony Van Dyck.   1632
*Hermitage, Leningrad*                                96

some Florentine dilettanti had attempted to revert to the musical ideals of antiquity by replacing the mannered contrapuntal methods of the Dutch with a monodic style of composition. When they produced, in 1597, at the house of one Jacopo Orsi, the operetta *Dafne*, with libretto by Ottavio Rinucinni and music by Jacopo Peri—a work consisting of recitative with a rather thin musical accompaniment—they thought they had really brought about a classical revival. This, however, was only the first step toward opera. Viadana and Monteverde were the real originators of the new style of music in which a euphonious body of sound was produced by a variety of instruments playing in concert. Opera arose in Italy, and first achieved popularity there, but roused equal enthusiasm as soon as it reached Germany. The court of Vienna never expended less than 10,000–15,000 gulden on every new opera; Munich lavished 70,000 gulden in 1662 on the production of *Medea*.[1] John George III, Elector

JOHANN GEORG AUS DEM
WINCKEL
Lucas Kilian. 1634

of Saxony, used to spend 8000 thalers a year on his private orchestra, and one of the Dukes of Hanover had an opera-house built which Lady Mary Wortley Montagu[2] considered far superior to that in Vienna. William Ernest, Duke of Saxe-Weimar, constructed one in the Wilhelmsburg;[3] before its inauguration in 1696, however, this noble lord discovered that the love of music conflicted with his sense of the devout, so

---

[1] *Medea vendicativa*, with libretto by Count Pietro Bissari of Vicenza and music by a composer now unknown, was one of three productions put on, at a cost of over 70,000 gulden, to celebrate the birth, on July 11, 1662, of Prince Max Emmanuel, heir to the Bavarian throne.

[2] 1689–1762, author of *Letters*.

[3] The ducal residence at Weimar, built in 1651; afterward destroyed by fire.

he compromised by opening the house with the opera *Von der denen lasterhaften Begierden entgegengesetzten tugendlichen Liebe* (*Virtuous Love versus Sinful Desire*). Not only at court was opera in Germany enthusiastically fostered; it secured its chief support at Hamburg, for here Senator Gerhard succeeded, in the face of violent clerical opposition, in erecting a permanent opera-house. It was inaugurated on January 2, 1678, with an opera by Christian Richter dealing with the creation, fall, and redemption of man, set to music by Theile. The cost of the enterprise ran into some 50,000 thalers a year; in Postel's opera *Die Eroberung Jerusalems* (*The Taking of Jerusalem*)[1] the expenses relating solely to the Temple of Solomon amounted to 15,000 thalers. During the first eighteen years sixty-three different operas were produced in Hamburg. Among those whose works obtained a hearing there were Lully, Handel, and the first German operatic composers, Heinrich Schütz and Reinhard Keiser; the latter composed 107 operas for Hamburg alone. Great care was lavished on the stage-setting; in Bostel's opera *Cara Mustapha*,[2] for instance, forty-eight different schemes of decoration were employed, for even in those days the scenic effect often aroused more interest than the music. Commenting on the French opera he attended in Amsterdam in 1687, Misson complains of the paucity of both machines and fine costumes, and in Venice, he says, there was nothing to see, and the opera was so dull it was difficult to sit it out.

In the seventeenth century there was no Press in our sense of the word. Newspapers existed, but their sole function was

**News-**  to circulate news. The German municipal autho-
**papers**  rities took the view expressed in 1697 by Stieler[3] that "it is undesirable to express opinions in newspapers." Germany preceded England and France in the development of a Press. While the earliest English weekly appeared in 1622, and a French one in 1631, the first weekly paper in Germany was published at Strassburg as early as 1605. The

---

[1] By Christian Heinrich Postel. The music for this opera was composed by Johann Georg Conradi.

[2] By Lukas von Bostel; music by Johann Wolfgang Francke.

[3] Caspar Stieler the poet, of Erfurt (1632–1707).

A FAMILY PARTY (PART)
Jan Miense Molenaer

first weekly to acquire a circulation of any note was the *Frankfurter Journal*, produced from 1615 onward at Frankfort-on-the-Main by Egenolf Emmel, but in the following year it had already found a competitor in the political notices issued by the Imperial postal administration of this city. Other

A FRENCH LADY
Solomon Savery

publications followed in course of time, but the practice of compiling news-letters by hand continued throughout the century. At Vienna, Nuremberg, Hamburg, Frankfort-on-the-Main, and other large centres of traffic scriveners were busily employed expediting by letter to the regular subscribers to their agencies all the news they could elicit from merchants, diplomats, and travellers. At Nuremberg, which boasted a central news market, the town council suffered considerable annoyance from these reporters. The pictorial Press of to-day owes its origin to Matthäus Merian, engraver and publisher, domiciled at Frankfort-on-the-Main. His extensive work, the *Theatrum Europæum*, contained "A True and Detailed Description of Each and Every Thing of Note, both Sacred and Profane, which has occurred throughout the World, but chiefly in Europe and Germany, from the year of Our Lord 1617 to 1713." The chronicler aimed at presenting, in his twenty-one mighty folio volumes, an historical chronicle of events, and thus furnished a companion work to the still more important production of his firm—the famous *Topographiæ*. In this work Merian has delineated all the characteristic parts of the German Fatherland, and has, in his truly delightful plates, left to posterity a faithful picture of

A FAMILY GROUP
Jan Miense Molenaer

seventeenth-century Germany. No comparable work exists in any other country.

As printed weeklies—dailies were only started in 1695, in England [1]—confined themselves to reporting news of vital and political interest, special literary journals were founded by scholars. The *Journal des Sçavans* was started in Paris in 1665, to be followed in 1668 by the *Giornale de' Letterati* in

IN THE SMOKING-ROOM
Jan Joris van Vliet

Rome, and in 1683 by the *Acta Eruditorum* in Germany. Public opinion, finding no outlet in newspapers, sought expression in innumerable pamphlets and broadsheets. In Germany, after the battle of the White Mountain,[2] a violent publicity campaign greatly aggravated the differences of the conflicting parties. The total number of broadsheets and pamphlets issued in England between the outbreak of the Civil War and the restoration of Charles II has been estimated at between 36,000 and 50,000.[3] In France, at the time of

---

[1] *The Postboy* was the first London daily, but only four numbers appeared.

[2] A site near Prague where the Protestant forces were defeated during the Thirty Years War (see p. 17, *n.* 2).

[3] Apparently an overestimate. *Cf.* G. K. Fortescue, *Catalogue of the Thomason Tracts, 1640–61* (British Museum, 1908), Introduction.

the Fronde,[1] this type of literature flourished apace; in one year nine hundred pamphlets directed against Mazarin appeared in Paris alone. Their rapid sale testified to the widespread unpopularity of this statesman. The enraged cardinal had all the libellous documents that he could lay hands upon confiscated, ostensibly to have them burned, and then proceeded to sell them secretly at high prices! During the reign of Louis XIV Holland flooded the European market with satires and lampoons. In Paris short work was made of both lampoonists and their publishers—they were sent to the gallows.

[1] A civil war which lasted from 1648 to 1652. The name (*fronde*, a sling) arose from the fact that the Paris mob slung stones at the windows of Cardinal Mazarin's adherents.

# CHAPTER III

## FASHIONS

THE dominant influence in the sixteenth century was Spain. When the seventeenth century dawned the world monarchy of Charles V was still intact,[1] but its internal strength was

MARTIN DAY
Rembrandt. 1634

sapped. The long reign of Philip II, with its disastrous domestic policy, had so thoroughly and permanently undermined the welfare of the country that even the immeasurable resources of the New World were bound to prove inadequate. Not the mother country alone, but the colonies of Spain too were ruined and laid waste by unsound administrative measures. To internal decay was added political defeat, and when, shortly before the dawn of the new century, Philip II closed his eyes a downfall could no longer have been averted, even by men of a very different calibre from Philip's son and grandson. It did, in fact, prove impossible to stop the decline which reduced the Spanish monarchy within less than a century from the rank of a world power to a helpless puppet in the hands of its rivals. During these years of decay in

---

[1] In point of fact, before the death of Philip II in 1598 Spain had lost Holland and given up Flanders.

which the social and political fabric of the State were crumbling art and poetry flourished. While Spain was forfeiting her place as a political power in the council of nations she was still endowing the world with untold wealth in the shape of men like Cervantes, Calderon, Velazquez, and Murillo.

Although, with her trade already ruined and her armies and fleets so often laid low, she was no longer feared, Spain continued to dominate social life with her fashions and mode of thought.

During the first two decades of the seventeenth century Spanish **Spanish** fashions still pre- **Dress** vailed abroad. In the third they began to make way for other modes, yet certain articles of Spanish costume resisted with extraordinary, almost incomprehensible, tenacity every change in style, and were retained not for decades but centuries. The chief characteristics of

MACHTELD VAN DOORN
Rembrandt. 1634

Spanish dress were a tightness and rigidity which impeded freedom of movement and forced the body into an unnatural position. The man's doublet, sleeves, and breeches were bombasted (see p. 47), and the only limb left outlined was the lower leg, which was encased in a stocking reaching midway up the thigh (see pp. 18, 31, 44). Still more falsifying was feminine dress, which confined the wearer within a basket-shaped skirt and stiff padded doublet in such a way that the shape of the figure was no longer even faintly discernible (see pp. 19, 25, 46, and plate facing p. 22). In both sexes the head was completely isolated from the rest of the

105

body by a stiff ruff of immense width (see pp. 23, 27, 38, 39, etc., and plate facing p. 44). The shape of the woman's body was further distorted by the steels of her corset, against the injurious effects of which the Swiss doctor Felix Platter protested in vain in 1602. Fashion achieved the barrel-shaped[1] effect of the lower part of the body by means of a thick bolster secured immediately above the hips (see p. 25), which, by causing the skirt first to stand out horizontally and then to fall in vertical lines to the ground, gave it so charac-

PORTRAIT OF A DUTCHWOMAN
Ferdinand Bol
*Photo F. Bruckmann A.-G., Munich*

teristic an appearance. The popular name in Germany for these farthingales was *Weiberspeck*.[2] They were so huge that Queen Margaret of Navarre was credited with having hers stuffed with the embalmed heads of her dead lovers, so that she might always feel these tender pledges of affection next to her 'heart.' These remarkable skirts remained in vogue for an incredible time. The Virgin Queen, Elizabeth of England (see p. 19), and Marie de Médicis, who was greatly her junior, both wore them, and they were universally adopted. State robes of princesses were not alone in displaying this cut: similar barrel-shaped figures distinguish the Dutch burgher women depicted in the *genre* pictures of fairs, sledging parties, and so on, painted by their countrymen (see pp. 35, 41). Spanish fashions were, more than any others, modes for the rich, for to set them off to proper advantage they required not only costly fabrics, such as heavy silks and velvets or gold and silver brocades, but adornment with jewels. Materials of different colour and kind were laid one over the other, and in order to display the under-material the upper one was slit,

---

[1] The barrel- or drum-shaped model was French, as opposed to the basket- or cone-shaped Spanish farthingale.

[2] *Weib*, woman; *Speck-* or *Schmerbauch*, paunch, pot-belly.

PORTRAIT OF A NOBLEMAN
Erasmus Quellinus
*Alte Pinakothek, Munich*

slashed, and pinked, and the made openings closed again with jewels (see pp. 53, 55). There is a portrait of Queen Elizabeth showing her in the famous toilet, smothered in brilliants, which she had made for the thanksgiving service held on November 24, 1588, to celebrate the destruction of the Armada (see p. 19). The robe worn by Marie de Médicis at the baptism on September 14, 1606, of Louis XIII and his sisters, Christine and Elizabeth, was trimmed with 32,000 pearls and 3000 diamonds. *Le Mercure de France*, in its account of a reception held at the Louvre in 1612, states that the garments of the Queen of Navarre and the Comtesse de Soissons were so thickly strewn with precious stones that the material was invisible. For the wedding of the Princess Elizabeth[1] with Frederick, Count Palatine—'the Winter King'[2]— Lady Arabella Stuart ordered a dress costing £1500, but instead of receiving an invitation, alas, she was locked up in the Tower.[3]

A LADY OF QUALITY
Jan van Ravesteyn. 1635

Masculine clothing made just as extravagant claims in respect of ornamentation as that of women. At the baptism of Louis XIII Marshal de Bassompierre wore a dress of cloth-of-gold trimmed with fifty pounds of real pearls. When the Duke of Buckingham (see p. 52) attended the nuptials of Charles I in Paris in 1625 the twenty-seven suits composing his wardrobe were trimmed with such costly embroideries, laces, and jewels that they were valued at 35,000 francs apiece, and the dress, closely studded with

[1] Daughter of James I.
[2] When Frederick accepted the crown of Bohemia the Jesuits prophesied that he would reign for only a winter. He did, in fact, retain the crown only from November 4, 1619, to November 8, 1620, the date of his defeat in the battle of the White Mountain (see p. 17, *n.* 2).
[3] For 'locked up' read 'left.' Lady Arabella was imprisoned from 1611 until her death in 1615. The wedding in question took place early in 1613.

diamonds, in which he appeared at the ceremony was worth 500,000 francs. And what does Ben Jonson say? "First, to be an accomplished gentleman, . . . 'twere good you turn'd four or five hundred acres of your best land into two or three trunks of apparel. . . ." [1] When King Sigismund III of Poland married the Archduchess Constantia in 1602 their wedding garments cost 700,000 thalers, and the court marshal who in 1626 conducted the Electoral Princess of Brandenburg to her bridegroom, Bethlen Gabor, Prince of Transylvania,

TWO GALLANTS AND A LADY
Jacques Callot. 1635

took with him for the occasion clothing to the value of 50,000 thalers. Henry, Prince of Wales, spent £2000 (about £10,000 in 1914 value) in one year on thirty-eight velvet, silk, and satin suits, and owned thirteen mantles, worth £50 apiece. The property of Hans Meinhard von Schönberg,[2] who died in 1616, included seventy-two costly suits, that of his wife thirty-two. Queen Elizabeth left at her death some two thousand sumptuous gowns, so the thrifty English Parliament, consisting, as it did, entirely of men, may be excused for decreeing that this wardrobe must suffice the new queen, Anne of Scotland, for the time, and that she had no need of new dresses. As a protest against the appalling extravagance to which such modes were leading, several noble families at Brunswick united in 1618 in a pledge never to permit any

[1] *Every Man out of his Humour.*
[2] German general and diplomat.

FASHION SHOPS IN THE GALLERY OF THE PALAIS-ROYAL

Abraham Bosse

of their members to wear a garment costing more than
200 thalers.

The most characteristic feature of Spanish dress was the
ruff—called in German a *Kröse*. It originated in the latter
**The**  part of the sixteenth century as successor to the
**Ruff**  tightly fitting shirt collar, and increased in size with
such rapidity that soon the handles of spoons had to be
lengthened to enable ladies and gentlemen to reach their
mouths. The main features of this ruff were its huge circum-
ference and board-like stiffness. There were several ways of
producing these. The material, consisting of either fine or
coarse linen, was goffered in narrow or wide tube-like sets
(see pp. 23, 49, and plate facing p. 44), or else caught together
along one edge and sewn into close sets (see p. 25). Yet other
ways were to arrange it in a number of superimposed layers
of flattened sets or of flat, fan-shaped folds (see pp. 42, 46).
As fashion required the ruff to project stiffly in all directions
its nickname of 'millstone'[1] was not inappropriate (see p. 39),
and as this stiffness could not be achieved solely by arranging
the material in thick layers additional means had to be sought.
So the pleats were wired inside, and light wire frames covered
in some thin material were worn under these thick ruffs as
a support.[2] Another means employed was starching, which
was developed into quite a fine art. A bluish starch,[3] made
from rice-flour, was the only one known at first, and was in
great vogue at the French court; Henry III tells us what
pleasure he derived from superintending the starching of his
own ruffs. A Mrs Turner then discovered a recipe for starch
which produced a yellow tint instead of a blue, and there was
great competition between the two colours. A political element even entered into the secrets of the wash-tub, the blue
starch being regarded as the mark of the Papist, the yellow
of the Huguenot. The yellow starch died a natural death
in 1615 after its lucky inventor had the misfortune to lose
both head and ruff for complicity in poisoning Sir Thomas

[1] Called the 'cartwheel' in England.
[2] In England this frame was known as the 'supportasse' or 'underpropper.'
[3] This 'bluish' starch may have been very similar to the 'white' starch we
use to-day, and the yellow starch mentioned later merely a cream tint.

HOME FROM THE CHRISTENING
Abraham Bosse

Overbury in the Tower. The Earl and Countess of Somerset, the real authors of the crime, escaped with banishment to their estates, but poor Mrs Turner had to ascend the scaffold. This she did in one of her famous yellow-starched ruffs, which went out of fashion from that day. Not only were ruffs made of the finest linen, but they were frequently edged throughout with lace, and were then immensely costly (see pp. 19, 42, 43, and frontispiece); a certain French courtier was not far wrong when he described himself as "wearing thirty-two acres of the best vineyard soil about my neck." [1]

Spanish dress was as uncomfortable as it was extravagant, condemning its wearers to hold themselves so stiffly that it can really only have been suitable for complete idlers. For workers, and people obliged to move about quickly and energetically, it was quite impracticable. As little by little all Europe succumbed to the fever of war, and for decade after decade Germany, France, England, and the Netherlands echoed with the clash of arms, Spanish costume gradually disappeared. Since soldiers could not possibly wear for any length of time garments into which they were stuffed like sausages in their skins or throttle themselves in ruffs that gave them stiff necks, masculine costume was the first to break away from the conventions of Spanish modes, and already in the first decade of the seventeenth century men's dress underwent changes tending toward greater comfort and freedom of movement. Women continued to follow the forms and cut of Spanish dress until midway between the twenties and thirties of the century, and even clung to the huge ruff for almost a generation after men had completely discarded it. Even then Spanish dress did not disappear entirely, for it was retained not only in its own country, but in countries politically dependent upon Spain. Veryard describes the Genoese in Spanish costume in 1682, and in 1688 Misson writes from Naples, "Every one here wears Spanish dress." Spanish fashions were also preserved by certain institutions which tend to lag behind the time—for instance, at court,

---

[1] For a useful article on ruffs see F. M. Kelly, in *The Burlington Magazine*, vol. 29, September 1916, pp. 245–250.

THE NURSERY
Abraham Bosse

in official and judicial offices, and in the pulpit. Daniel L'Hermite,[1] who saw Rudolph II shortly before this Emperor's death, remarks that he was dressed quite in the old style. Until the first Lorrainer, in the person of Francis I, mounted the throne, the court of the Vienna Habsburgs always donned Spanish dress for ceremonial occasions. Certain rudiments of this dress, above all the great ruff, were even preserved by the patriciate of the German Imperial cities throughout the eighteenth century, and are still retained in present-day official garments at Bremen, Hamburg, and Lübeck.

Masculine clothing now veered in the opposite direction from Spanish costume with its general narrowness and tight-

**Masculine Costume** ness, and acquired a wide, loose—vulgarly speaking, sloppy—character. The main difference lay in the breeches; formerly short, round, and bombasted, reaching barely midway down the thigh (see pp. 18, 44), they now became long and ample. They were still drawn together at the hem, but came to the knee now, below which they were fastened. The bands employed for this purpose were like narrow scarves, and were trimmed with long lace ends (see pp. 28, 30, 32, 58, 60, 61, and plate facing p. 56).[2] The material, once slashed lengthways, was now left whole, or at most slit down the outer seam to display the underlinen, in which case a favourite style was to finish the breeches off at the knee with a ribbon rosette (see pp. 57, 58, 63). The upper garments had hitherto been two in number—the sleeved doublet and the *Koller*,[3] the latter being either sleeveless or provided with ornamental hanging sleeves, and being worn over the doublet (see pp. 21, 24, 62, 67, 70, and plate facing p. 114). The skirts which provided an extension below the waist to the doublet and *Koller* were laced on—that is to say, they were attached by means of small loops ending in metal tags (see pp. 58, 62, and plate facing p. 64).[4] These skirts

---

[1] Or l'Ermite.

[2] According to Frithjof van Thienen, *Das Kostüm der Blütezeit Hollands, 1600–60* (1930), these bands were not used to hold the breeches in, but the stockings up.

[3] Comparable to the English jerkin of that time. *Cf.* the *Goller* or *Koller* of the sixteenth century in *Modes and Manners*, vol. ii, p. 139.

[4] Most experts are of opinion that the points secured the skirts of the doublet to the breeches beneath them, to hold them up, and not to the body of the doublet.

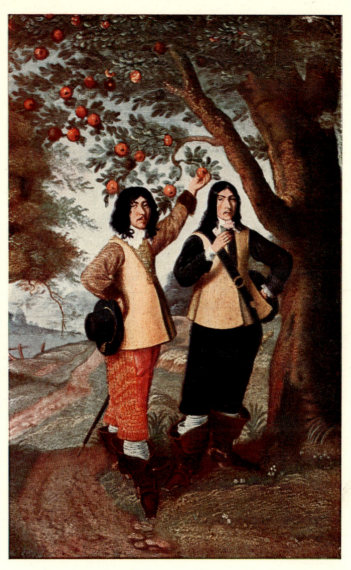

SMELL AND TASTE
From a representation of the Five Senses
Unknown master

*Von Lipperheide Library of Costume, Berlin*          114

THE SHOEMAKER
Abraham Bosse

were not made in a single piece, but consisted of a number of flaps broadening out at the base so that they overlapped one another, and covered the lower part of the trunk. Doublet and *Koller* now very gradually altered in shape until, in the latter part of the century, they assumed—as waistcoat and coat—the forms still favoured by the masculine world to-day. The chief change came when the doublet surrendered its sleeves to the *Koller*, which, with skirts no longer attached[1] in separate pieces, but long, and cut in front in one with the body, was now turned into a coat. This long-tailed, sleeved coat, which made its appearance in the fashionable world at the beginning of the thirties, was already known among peasants before that time. Apart from unimportant details, the coat worn at Breitenfeld by Tilly (see p. 73) exactly resembled in cut that seen fifty years later on Louis XIV (*cf.* pp. 172, 214). Its appearance in the interval was only spasmodic, but in the same way that this coat first saw life in combatant circles so its reappearance was largely due to the exigencies of military life. The change in the shape of breeches was accompanied by a change in footwear. The low shoe which went with the close-fitting trunk-hose of Spanish costume (see pp. 18, 31, 44, 48, 50) made way for the top-boot, which in its early days rose to the knee. Later it was shortened to reach only to the middle of the calf, and the top was widened out like a funnel and lined with a loose gaiter of linen or batiste or—still better—with lace (see pp. 57-59, 62, 67, 70, 93, 101, etc., and plate facing p. 114). The latter provided scope for great extravagance. Cinq-Mars, the unfortunate favourite of Louis XIII, deprived of his beautiful head by Richelieu in 1642, left three hundred pairs of lace trimmings for riding-boots. Those who still preferred shoes adorned them in front with lace roses (see pp. 58, 60, 61, 94-96, 104, 117, etc., and plate facing p. 56), also no cheap ornament! In England, according to Peacham, their price varied from 30*s.* to £5; he even mentions a pair that had cost £30 (about £150 in 1914 value),[2] and a Puritan in the

---

[1] *Cf.* p. 114, *n.* 4.
[2] Henry Peacham the Younger, *The Truth of our Times* (1638).

HEARING

From a series of the Five Senses

Abraham Bosse

House of Commons maintained with pretty exaggeration that shoe roses cost a son more than his father was once wont to pay for his whole suit. With low shoes were worn silk stockings of varying shades (see plates facing pp. 136, 142); in 1612 the wardrobe of the Earl of Rutland contained flesh-coloured, green, grey, silver, and black stockings.

Not until changes in neck- and head-gear were involved, and especially not until the great ruff took its departure, was the transformation complete. This huge, stiff, awkward ruff proved such a nuisance that it underwent alteration even while the other items of Spanish costume were still retained. It was not discarded, but the practice of starching it was discontinued, and it was allowed to fall in close, soft folds. This more comfortable but not exactly becoming article of apparel may be seen in a number of contemporary pictures (see pp. 67, 101, and plate facing p. 64). In the famous *Anatomy Lesson of Professor Tulp*, painted by Rembrandt in 1632, only one of the students has on a stiff ruff; the six others all wear soft, unstarched ones (see p. 74). Charles I of England adopted the new style of ruff in the fourth year of his reign, but could not, according to Evelyn, induce bishops or judges to follow suit. Others discarded the ruff altogether in favour of a narrow linen band falling over the collar of the doublet, not unlike the Eton collar of to-day;[1] Tulp, in Rembrandt's picture, is wearing a collar of this kind. Others, again, were content with the plain, small stiffened collar formerly worn only as a support beneath the great ruff (see pp. 48, 153, and plate facing p. 82). This plate-shaped collar owed its fame to the fact that it

The Golilla

was—under the name of *golilla*[2]—not merely the only fashionable collar in Spain, but, after the wearing of lace was prohibited in 1623, the only collar permitted by law. With three exceptions, the numerous portraits of Philip IV executed by Velazquez between 1623 and 1660 show his royal master in this collar. When Charles I went to Madrid to sue for the hand of the Infanta Maria he appeared at court

[1] *Cf.* our 'falling band.'
[2] Diminutive of the Spanish *gola* ('gullet' or 'gorget').

**BLOOD-LETTING**
Abraham Bosse

THE FOOLISH VIRGINS ASLEEP
Abraham Bosse

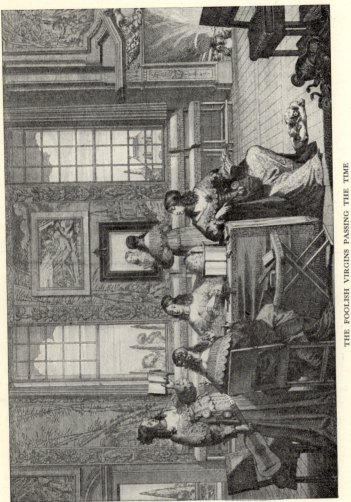

THE FOOLISH VIRGINS PASSING THE TIME

Abraham Bosse

in the strictly prohibited ruff until the Duchess de Olivares ensured his correct attire by presenting him with a *golilla*. His companion on this occasion—the Duke of Buckingham (see p. 52)—immediately had himself painted by Rubens in 1625 resplendent in a *golilla*. Alongside these types there gradually established itself the soft, wide lace collar (see pp. 76, 78, 85, 87-89, 96, etc.), an early example of which occurs in the portrait of the artist and his wife painted by Rubens in 1610 (see p. 23). Such favour did this elegant collar find that after the thirties it ousted all other styles and reigned supreme. Until then positive anarchy had ruled in the world of collars (see p. 35). In 1601, for instance, the album of Katharina von Canstein was enriched by portraits of two brothers von der Asseburg—Heinrich in a large ruff, Johann in a small Eton collar. The pictures in Pluvinel[1] of Louis XIII at his riding lessons show the young King and his attendants sometimes in the starched, sometimes in the soft ruff, and quite frequently in the *golilla*. Similar variety may be observed in the series of etchings depicting Girard Thibault at Leyden in the act of giving fencing instruction.[2]

The change in collars was naturally accompanied by a change in coiffure and hats. The stiff ruff, tilting up at the back, had practically compelled men to have short-cut hair (see plate facing p. 44), but with its disappearance this necessity vanished. The falling band now had the effect of a magnet on men's hair. Their heads suddenly became framed in a mass of hair (see, for example, p. 57, plate facing p. 96); sometimes it floated in a tangle of unkempt strands (see p. 87, and plate facing p. 114), sometimes curled in beautifully dressed locks, which came to just over the ear on the right side of the face, but fell on to the shoulder on the left (see p. 58 *et seq.*). This long piece consisted either in one loose curl or in a braided tress, or else the hair was just bound together (see pp. 81, 82, 123). The name given to it, after Honoré d'Albert, Seigneur de Cadenet

*Hair and Hats*

---

[1] Crispin van de Passe II engraved the plates for the famous treatise on horsemanship issued by Antoine de Pluvinel in 1623.

[2] Girard Thibault, *L'Espée de Girard Thibault : la théorie et pratique du maniement des armes* (1628).

THE SECOND WIFE OF SEBASTIAN LEERSE
Anthony Van Dyck
*Alte Pinakothek, Munich*

122

TASTE

From a series of the Five Senses

Abraham Bosse

(brother of Constable de Luynes, the favourite of Louis XIII), was *cadenette*.[1] Besides possessing very lovely fair hair, de Cadenet is said to have been the first to curl it in this way and to think of braiding it with 'favours' in the form of gay ribbons or small jewels whose chief value lay in the fact that they were the gift of some fair lady. Some of Germany's folk-songs as recorded toward the middle of the century twit young men with purchasing these favours and then bragging that they had received them as love-tokens. This coquettish coiffure was by no means a monopoly of young bloods; portraits of Christian IV as an old man show the glum and homely countenance of the Danish King with a pearl-adorned pigtail framing his ear. The Comte d'Harcourt, a sprig of the house of Lorraine, acquired his nickname of Cadet la Perle from the pearl in his hair (see p. 81). Now since everybody did not rejoice in a natural abundance of hair, almost simultaneously with the adoption of the lace collar appeared the periwig (see, for example, pp. 82, 84, 117, 119, 123, 163, 169).

The Periwig   As early as 1615 travellers reported that they had seen in Paris gentlemen wearing over their own hair false heads of hair, which they called periwigs. In 1624 the prematurely bald Louis XIII also decided to don a periwig, and thereafter this coiffure remained in vogue for a couple of centuries. The new style of hairdressing called so imperiously for a new style of hat that the small, high-crowned hat—the *Barett* of Spanish fashions in Germany [2]—now made way for the large, pliable felt hat with broad brim and sweeping plumes (see, for example, pp. 62, 64, 67, 79, 82, 95, and plate facing p. 150). *Respondent* [3] was a good name for it, for by the various ways in which the brim could be bent —either up over the ears or down over the face—it could be adapted to express the mood of its wearer.

These, then, were the garments in which men, radically changed from head to foot, appeared toward 1630—the

---

[1] 'Lovelock.'

[2] The Spanish *Barett* was not unlike our Beefeater's hat, and preceded, in Germany, the high-crowned Spanish hat. See *Modes and Manners*, vol. ii, especially p. 152.

[3] The German verb *respondieren* can mean 'to adapt itself to.'

**SIGHT**

From a series of the Five Senses

Abraham Bosse

approximate starting-point of universal fashions. Thereafter free fancy in dress ceased, and both national and local peculiarities disappeared; fashion was dictated by one inexorable law, and long before the seventeenth century took wing high society in every land had abandoned all initiative in this field,

CARDINAL RICHELIEU
Philippe de Champaigne

and was everywhere clothing itself with a scrupulous and eager eye to French modes. It is at about this time that Abraham a Sancta Clara writes caustically, in his *Welt-Galleria* (*Universal Gallery*), "Rarely did any country dress like another, until some few years back Parisian modes spread like a perfect cancer, and now a number of nations are infected by the disease."

Women clung with far greater tenacity than men to Spanish dress. Long after man had escaped from the tyranny of

THE ARTIST'S WEDDING
David Teniers the Younger

Spanish modes women still wore the stiffened bodice, huge millstone ruff, and stiff, barrel-like skirt (see pp. 96, 106, 107,

Feminine 145, 148, 149, and plate facing p. 90). In Katharina
Costume von Canstein's family album her kinswomen[1] and others appear until well into the thirties of the century in all the rigid pomp of a costume resembling point for point, not only in cut but in its surfeit of jewels, the attire of Queen Elizabeth. And here the truth must out—the dazzling wealth

DRAWINGS BY WENZEL HOLLAR

of precious stones so frequently seen in pictures of this time were by no means always the property of the sitter. Often the artist, with excess of zeal, endowed his models with riches which they did not possess in fact. When, for example, English ladies had themselves painted they had to pay ten shillings extra if they wished the artist to depict them in a fine string of pearls. Lady Sussex wrote once to Lord Verney that Van Dyck had adorned her portrait far too lavishly with diamonds —she had not nearly so many.

The first change of any real note in feminine dress was the abandonment of the great hip-pad (see p. 25). The skirt then fell in far more graceful folds, and the figure somewhat recovered its human contour. A flow of line far more akin

<hr />

[1] A string of unimportant names is quoted here in the original.

SIGNING THE MARRIAGE CONTRACT
Miniature by Abraham Bosse. 1633
*Kaiser Friedrich Museum, Berlin*

to nature took the place of the conventional figure induced by Spanish modes. But the eye, which had been accustomed for so many decades to seeing women with an absurdly augmented hip measurement, demanded a transition stage, and therefore fashion, which never moves by leaps and bounds but only step by step, compromised at first by bunching the skirt up all round to about half its original length, and securing it at the waist (see pp. 27, 28, 64, 67, and plate facing p. 70). Lining and underskirt were now visible, and provided fine opportunities for extravagant display. It was customary to wear, apart from the dress, three petticoats, each of a different colour. These petticoats were styled by the French *la secrète* ('the hidden'), *la modeste* ('the chaste'), and *la friponne* ('the rogue'). The beautiful Gabrielle d'Estrées owned petticoats of cloth-of-gold flowered in blue, red, and green, Marie de

HÉLÈNE FOURMENT
Peter Paul Rubens

Médicis underskirts of white satin lined with green taffeta, yellow satin lined with red silk, and black satin worked in gold flowers. Ladies compelled by circumstances to select less magnificent materials usually managed to trim their petticoats with lace or galloon them in gold. So it is easy to understand the indignation of the Countess Ulfeldt when upon her removal to the Copenhagen prison she was deprived of her silk petticoat with gold lace trimming and given instead a linen one ornamented with only a pinked pattern. The greatest extravagances in respect of petticoats were committed by Spanish ladies, who, to the amazement of their elegant French sisters, wore seven or eight of these garments in the summer and twelve or more in the winter, all of them made of heavy, costly material lavishly trimmed with gold or silver lace, and thus often valued at 500 or 600 kronen apiece. Only the bottom petticoat—called *sabenagua*[1] in Spanish—was of linen, and a lady never owned more than one, and had to stay in bed when it needed washing.

GEORGE DIGBY, EARL OF BRISTOL, AND
WILLIAM RUSSELL, EARL OF BEDFORD
Anthony Van Dyck

When the skirt was not bunched up in the manner referred to by Mrs Earle as "washerwoman style"[2] it parted in front over the petticoat, again bringing this garment into evidence (see pp. 55, 63, 90). The skirt, deprived now of its hip-bolster and stiffening, became long enough to sweep the ground and even developed a train (see, for example, pp. 98, 101, 109). Since for Spanish ladies to show their feet was a mortal sin they wore all their dresses long enough to tread on, a feat requiring special instruction and practice. The change in the skirt was accompanied by changes in the bodice. The high-necked bodice of Spanish fashion, lacing into a long point, and with puffed and padded sleeves (see pp.

[1] Clearly quoted from the Comtesse d'Aulnoy's *Voyage d'Espagne*, in which work the editor of the edition published in 1926 in the *Revue Hispanique* adds a footnote, "Read: *enagua*." Properly the word should read *enaguas* (skirt or petticoat). Its diminutive, *enagüillas*, also means petticoat. Both forms are plural.

[2] "I see that they [Puritan women] gather up their gowns for walking after a mode known in later years as washerwoman style."—Alice M. Earle, *Two Centuries of Costume* (1903), p. 89.

19, 46), was exchanged for one of less severe style terminating in its natural place below the bust (see p. 136). The neck opening was cut very low, but filled in again with a collar of batiste or lace (see pp. 90, 93, 136, and plate facing p. 122).

VISCOUNT GRANDISON
Pieter van Gunst, after Anthony Van Dyck

When the great ruff is still seen on men in portraits later than the early thirties it may be taken to represent a token of office (see pp. 91, 160); on women, however, it is found until the sixties. After 1632 Rembrandt painted only two ecclesiastics in ruffs—quite small ones at that—while as late as 1661 he portrayed a lady in a great cartwheel ruff. The Städel Art Gallery at Frankfort-on-the-Main contains a picture by Franz

Hals of a lady aged forty-four still wearing a large ruff in 1678. During these years when the ruff was, so to speak, fighting for its existence it increased in both height and breadth to dimensions as preposterous as those attained by ladies' hats to-day.[1] A portrait by Van Dyck at Lille Museum shows a lady arrayed in a ruff of amazing height, and Rembrandt's Fru van Beeresteyn is wearing one the size of

QUEEN HENRIETTA MARIA
Godfrey Kneller, after Anthony Van Dyck
*Photo F. Bruckmann A.-G., Munich*

a cartwheel, extending from shoulder to shoulder. But the days of the ruff were numbered; it was now cherished only by the older generation, who continued to abide by Spanish modes. The stiff ruff was entirely unsuitable to the light, natural style of clothing now in vogue, and still more so to the rapidly spreading fashion of low dress. The lace collar known as the Stuart collar [*sic*],[2] which formed a screen round the back of the neck, was retained until the thirties (see pp. 45, 60, 65, and plate facing p. 156). It left the throat bare, and made a pleasing frame to the head. Rubens painted Jacqueline de Castres in 1617, the Countess of Arundel in 1620, and Hélène Fourment in 1630 (see p. 69) in collars of this kind; Isabella Brant, portrayed in 1623, and Suzanne Fourment, in about 1623, are wearing considerably smaller ones. This collar finally came to lie flat, either softening the neck opening or filling it in (see, for example, pp. 95, 109–113, and plate facing p. 76). Ladies and gentlemen wore lace collars identical in style (see pp. 109, 117, 119, and plates facing pp. 128, 136, 150), and it was an act of the utmost gallantry when Gustavus Adolphus (see p. 76), at the dance given in his honour by

---

[1] This book was first published in German in 1913.
[2] This was the *collet montant*, or 'upright collar.'

the city of Augsburg in 1632, paid tribute to Jacobine Lauber as the belle of the ball by unclasping his collar (see p. 78) and placing it round her neck.

The elegance of the bodice was determined by the cut of the sleeves, which grew wider and wider (see p. 111, and plates facing pp. 122, 128) and could be arranged in innumerable ways. In an old English comedy of the period, *The Maid in the Mill*,[1] a tailor says to the maid,

QUEEN HENRIETTA MARIA
Anthony Van Dyck
*Photo F. Bruckmann A.-G., Munich*

> Oh, sleeve, oh, sleeve! I'll
>   study all night, madam,
> To magnify your sleeve.

While formerly the material was slashed and disposed up the arm in a series of padded puffs (see pp. 25, 46), now it was just loosely puffed and held in at elbow and wrist with a ribbon bow (see pp. 53, 69, 94).[2] This type of sleeve occurs in the portraits of Anna Wake, Mme Le Roy, and many other Van Dyck portraits of the twenties. Hairdressing displayed a similar tendency toward a looser, lighter style. Spanish fashions had decreed that the hair should be dressed high on the head and set in tight curls round temples and brow (see frontispiece and plate facing p. 90); it was now parted so that the front portion fell on either side of the face in long ringlets, the remainder being braided in a knot on the crown of the head (see pp. 121, 161). Frequently it was damped and powdered. Ladies and gentlemen also applied patches to their faces. In 1616 Count Christoph von Dohna saw at the court of Berlin some ladies heavily made up and plastered in patches, which they called *lustres*.[3] We

[1] By John Fletcher, produced in 1623, printed in 1647.
[2] There was usually a lace cuff at the wrist.
[3] 'Foils'—*i.e.*, to beauty.

have also the testimony of Moscherosch. "I saw," writes he scoffingly,

> a crowd of women looking as though they had had their faces scratched, pecked and cut, for on all the parts to which they desired to attract attention were stuck small black plasters in the shape of gnats and fleas of every imaginable shape and size as well as of other singular lures to finger and eye.

In England patches do not seem to have been known until somewhat later, for Bulwer first mentions them in 1650; apart

THE COUNTESS OF DORSET
Anthony Van Dyck

from stars, crescent moons, and the like, he describes a patch in the form of a coach and pair which ladies wore on the brow.[1] Men affected patches in England too.

By about 1640 the transformation in ladies' fashions was likewise complete; every article of costume had then acquired an easy, flowing line, for the frames and pads which made them so stiff had vanished (see pp. 119-121). The cut of feminine dress, with its fairly wide, plain skirt and short, low-necked bodice, had now made considerable strides toward simplicity and grace. For some time longer—possibly by reason of the influence exerted by the women of the Dutch burgher class—fashion continued to follow these lines. Holland was then at the zenith of her political power and enjoying immense wealth, circumstances ample to account for the influence wielded by this country in social matters; that this influence also extended to the world of fashion may well have been because between 1630 and 1660 [sic] there was no European court capable of setting the modes. The courts of Vienna and Madrid

[1] John Bulwer, *Anthropometamorphosis, or The Artificial Changeling* (1650).

are beside the mark, as they not only continued to follow Spanish fashions, but, in the case of feminine dress, exaggerated them to the point of caricature; at the French court the Queen-Regent Anne of Austria was in widow's weeds; the court of St James's was dispersed, and its Queen and princes were eating the bread of exile. It is not difficult, therefore, to

DRAWING BY JACOB OCHTERVELT
*Print Room of the Berlin Museums*

account for the widespread popularity achieved by the attire of the wealthy and cultured citizenesses of Holland. The mode of covering neck and bosom with wide, semi-transparent collars of fine linen or batiste (see pp. 93, 99, 136) was directly due to the Dutch fashion, with its increasing tendency toward simplicity in dress,[1] and the Dutch exerted a similar influence on colour, for black was rapidly becoming the fashionable wear (see plates facing pp. 70, 172). Formerly a motley costume spelt elegance, and there was nothing unusual in

[1] *I.e.*, in contour.

wearing ten or twelve shades together. "A painter has not
as many colours on his palette as the Frenchman in his dress,"
wrote Marini[1] from Paris to Cardinal Montalto; in 1608 the
Englishman Coryate[2] was reproaching his countrymen on
similar grounds. But the craze now was for more neutral
tones and broken colours ("pale blue, light red, light green,
neutral yellow, neutral green—hybrid colours, because they

present an appearance of doubtful honour," says Moscherosch
wrathfully), above all for black.
The striking feature of seventeenth-century portraits is that
most of the sitters are wearing
black—as if this century, lying
between two such colourful ones
as the sixteenth and eighteenth,
felt impelled to vouchsafe the
eye an interval of repose after
the one and before the next
orgy of colour. Coloured clothing eventually became so un-
common that in the time of
Louis XIV the days 'when

PORTRAIT OF THE ARTIST
Anna Maria van Schurmann. 1640

people still wore colours' were spoken of as of some remote
past almost beyond living memory. Dutch women also
introduced into the feminine wardrobe that practical and
comfortable article of dress known to modern times as a
*matinée*.[3] In the Dutch interiors by Mieris, Netscher, van
der Neer, Jan Steen, Ter Borch, and others nearly all the
young women and girls appear in these semi-*négligés*, most of
which, if the painter's brush may be trusted, were apparently
made of silk or velvet trimmed with fur.

. While feminine fashions were progressing on sensible and
practical lines masculine modes were reaching heights of

---

[1] Perhaps Giovanni Battista Marini (1569–1625), Italian poet.
[2] Thomas Coryate (1577(?)–1617), English traveller and writer. *Coryate's
Crudities*, an account of a walking tour undertaken in 1608, here referred to, was
published in 1611.
[3] A jacket.

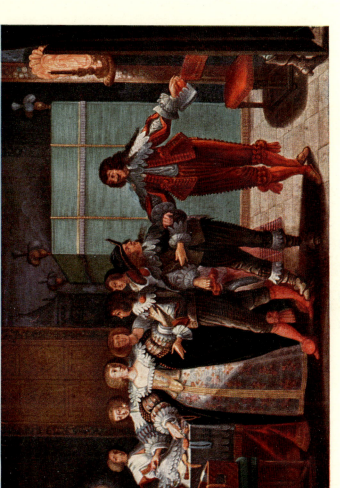

THE WEDDING NIGHT

Miniature by Abraham Bosse.   1633

*Kaiser Friedrich Museum, Berlin*

136

extravagance seldom attained before and never since. A costume more effeminate and unpractical than that affected by men between about 1635 and 1660 would be hard to devise. By combining in one garment the sleeves of the doublet and the skirts of the *Koller* (see p. 116) a new coat-like garment was evolved. These skirts, formerly consisting of flaps (see p. 70), were now cut in one piece, and

Men's Dress 1635-60

any points introduced on the coat served solely as ornament. As soon as trimming was dispensed with and points discarded, and when sleeves were no longer slashed, the coat produced bore a remarkable resemblance to the modern jacket (see p. 116 and pp. 130, 131). Several of the portraits painted by Van Dyck in the late thirties—that of Arthur Goodwin, for instance—show a coat not so different from that of to-day; as already at that date we find on gentlemen of fashion narrow breeches reaching nearly to the ankles, it is, indeed, permissible to say that jacket and trousers, the man's present-day suit, existed before. This jacket made only a very short stay, how-

AN ENGLISH LADY
Wenzel Hollar. 1639

ever, for no sooner did it appear than fashion, with its constant tendency to extremes [*sic*], took it in hand and turned a practical garment into a perfect absurdity. Not only did gentlemen no longer close their coat right down the front, but it was shortened and the sleeves were reduced to about half their original length, so that it looked exactly like a child's jacket. At the same time breeches changed; they became, though only for a while, narrower in cut and were left loose at the hem (see pp. 82, 84, 91, 128). Elegance depended less upon costly fabrics than upon trimming, and upon a wonderful array of white linen; the shirt had become one of the main objects of luxury, thus denoting greater refinement in taste. Male attire permitted a vast expanse of this garment to show,

137

for with an open coat that barely covered the ribs the shirt was visible, not only right down the front but to the breadth of a couple of hands round the waist, and almost the whole of its wide sleeves was displayed (see pp. 166, 179, 180). As even this did not satisfy some beaux the handsome, blond Gaston de Nogaret, Duc de Candale, conceived the notion of cutting the top of the breeches down to the hip line. The shirt then showed to the breadth of

AN ENGLISH LADY
Wenzel Hollar. 1640

some three hands, and men looked as though they were losing their breeches. It was only natural that an article of dress by which such store was set should be magnificently trimmed, and gentlemen's shirts were, in fact, lavishly adorned with lace insertions, collar, and cuffs. The inventory of the Earl of Rutland's wardrobe in 1612 records twenty-one plain and nineteen lace-trimmed shirts, and at the palace of Rosenborg [1] may still be seen the laced shirts of King Christian IV of Denmark. Charles I of England once purchased 1000 yards of lace for trimming twelve shirts and over 600 for his nightshirts. In London in 1638 a man's collar could not be had under £3 or £4 (£15 to £20 in 1914 value). Not only hands but knees were encircled with lace frills (see pp. 91, 109, 117, 131). Knee-frills, called *canons* in France,[2] could cost up to 7000 livres[3] a pair. At the French court, says M. d'Alquié,[4] it was not unusual for a nobleman to expend 13,000 livres on a lace set consisting of collar, cuffs, and knee-frills.

[1] In Copenhagen.

[2] The English 'cannon' or 'post-cannon.' F. M. Kelly (*Historic Costume*, 1929) warns against confusing it with the 'canion' of *c.* 1570, an extension to the knee of the trunk-hose.

[3] The livre of 20 sous was approximately equivalent to the pre-War (1914) franc.

[4] François-Savinien d'Alquié, writer, flourished in the latter part of the seventeenth century.

Toward the middle of the thirties—probably as a result of the French edicts of 1633 and 1634 prohibiting gold and silver embroideries—lace was followed by trimming in the form of ribbons (see pp. 82, 84). The now wide breeches were finished off round knees and waist with ribbon loops, which also ran in a tapering line down the middle of the front. Nor was the jacket neglected, but was adorned here, there, and everywhere with loops. Michel de Marolles reckoned 300 metres of ribbon for a gentleman's

*Ribbon Trimmings*

ENGRAVING FROM "LA SCHERMA DI FRANCESCO FERNANDO ALFIERI"
Padua, 1640

suit—a modest amount, really, considering that in 1656 a man of fashion in France had to have some five or six hundred loops upon his person (see pp. 169, 186, 188). A Saxon police regulation of 1661 attests to the fact that 200 or more ells of silk ribbon constituted quite a normal trimming; it aimed at restricting future amounts to 50 ells of taffeta ribbon for a nobleman, 30 for a *bourgeois*, and 10 or 15 at most for one of the lower orders. "It was a fine silken thing which I spied walking th'other day through Westminster Hall, that had as much Ribbon about him as would have plundered six shops, and set up twenty country Pedlers; all his body was drest like a May-pole," writes John Evelyn.[1] "To see the way in which their breeches and doublets are transformed and disguised, festooned and draped, caught up and decked

[1] In *Tyrannus, or The Mode* (1661), reprinted in *Memoirs* (first edition, 1818), pp. 323 ff.

with all manner of rags and tags, laces and loops, one might think one was inspecting a haberdasher's shop," are the words in which Moscherosch, in his *Schergenteuffel*,[1] pokes fun at the men.

Midway through the century was introduced the rhinegrave —breeches resembling a petticoat in cut. This style originated in Holland, was introduced in Paris by the Wald-grave [2] and Rhinegrave von Salm, and immediately became the rage. These breeches usually consisted of some 20 to 30 metres of material made into a short undivided skirt that reached to the knees (see pp. 166, 172, 179, 186, 189, 197, 199, and plate facing p. 180). The first description of them as petticoat-breeches occurs in 1688 from the pen of the Englishman Randle Holme,[3] but the fashion must have spread very quickly, for in 1662 a sumptuary law of the city of Dresden prohibited their wear by journeymen, and in 1663 Pastor Ouw delivered a thundering philippic against them from a Flensburg pulpit. The rhinegrave was first depicted as gentleman's attire in the pictures issued in 1628 from his fencing-school by Girard Thibault, fencing-master at the University of Leyden.[4] By 1680 it must already have been out of fashion, for Lisclotte, who once remarked, "The rhinegrave suits people with good figures," then announces that the Margrave of Ansbach has made a laughing-stock of himself at Versailles by appearing in this garment. The pronouncement of *Le Mercure de France*, "Cannons and rhinegraves are impossible," rang their final death-knell in 1682. These

The Rhine-grave

---

[1] See p. 36, n. 2. The *Schergenteuffel* is a part of his best-known work *Wunderliche . . . Gesichte Philanders von Sittewalt* (Sittewald) (1644–45).

[2] This old German title, used especially in the Rhineland, stood for *comes silvester*, 'overseer of the woods.'

[3] Author of *The Academy of Armoury*, in which this description occurs; but possibly Thomas Reeve, in his earlier *God's Plea for Nineveh* (1657, p. 124)— "some [men] walk (as it were) in their Wastcoats, and others (a man would think) in their Petticoats"—refers to the same article of clothing.

[4] It is difficult to distinguish the very wide breeches of those days from the rhinegrave, but Frithjof van Thienen, in *Das Kostüm der Blütezeit Hollands, 1600–60* (1930), states that the rhinegrave was the name for the skirt and trunk-hose combined, as seen in the illustration at p. 197, and that even if Salm introduced it at Versailles it was not of Dutch origin. There is no sign of a rhinegrave in Thibault's work here referred to (for title see p. 122, n. 2), only of wide breeches.

AN EVENING PARTY
Bartholomäus Wittig. 1640
Photo F. Bruckmann A.-G., Munich

petticoat-breeches had, however, remained the approved garment of the masculine world of fashion for nearly thirty years, and enjoyed as generous a share of ribbon trimming as ordinary breeches. This costume, which all but bordered on feminine dress, found such favour with the ladies that they also adopted it. A picture in Buckingham Palace shows the Duchess of Richmond in a rhinegrave, and in 1672 the Duchess of Portsmouth ordered herself a man's suit the detailed account for which is still in existence. The tailor used 10 ells of dove-grey silk, and to trim the suit 108 ells of scarlet silk ribbon, 22 ells of silver lace, and six dozen silver buttons, the bill totalling over £59 (about £300 in 1914 value).[1] Trimming became madly extravagant. Duke Frederick of Schomberg once had two suits made, one of velvet, one of cloth, each heavily embroidered, and the only part of the material that remained plain—a strip about an inch wide—was trimmed with lace. John Evelyn, on witnessing the progress of Louis XIV to Parliament on September 7, 1651, wrote, "The King himself like a young Apollo, was in a sute so cover'd with rich embrodry, that one could perceive nothing of the stuff under it." To Lady Fanshawe[2] we owe the description of the garments in which her husband, as Charles II's ambassador, had his first audience of Philip IV of Spain. He wore, she says, a dark brocade suit laced with nine bands of gold and silver lace, a hand's-breadth wide, with narrower bands of such lace between them, the trimming consisting of scarlet taffeta ribbands. With this he wore long scarlet silk stockings under loose white silk ones. The jewel on his hat was worth £1200, and the gold chain about his neck bearing a miniature of the King set in diamonds £300.

The French called the ribbon loops on a gentleman's dress *galants*,[3] and the *ensemble* of the trimming *petite-oie*.[4] In 1677 M. de la Basinière boasted 250 metres of ribbon in his *petite-oie*.

The finishing touches to this remarkable costume were supplied by the periwig and shoes. Fashion, which insisted

[1] The suit is said to have been ordered for wearing at a masque.
[2] In her *Memoirs*, written in 1676 and first published in 1829.
[3] The *galants* marked the dress of the fop or beau (*le galant*).
[4] Literally, the accessory parts or giblets of a goose: the accessories of dress.

THE APOTHECARY AT A SICK-BED
Miniature by Abraham Bosse
*Kaiser Friedrich Museum, Berlin*

142

upon long hair for men, obliged even the Sun-King to don a
wig when his lovely blond locks began to get thin.    The
For a long time he would not hear of it, and not    Periwig

WILLIAM II, PRINCE OF ORANGE, AND HIS BRIDE, PRINCESS MARY
Attributed to Anthony Van Dyck (? Adriaen Hanneman).  1641

until 1673, at the age of thirty-five, did Louis XIV take to
false hair (see pp. 169, 171, 177, 178, 214).  The periwig had
received official sanction when this French king in 1655
appointed forty-eight court periwig-makers at a stroke, and
in 1656 established their first guild in Paris.  During the early

years of the century the periwig resembled a natural head of long locks, though young bloods favoured a curly shock. The colour preferred was blond, for men then cherished the pretty conceit that they looked like lions. A blond wig made with human hair cost from 2000 to 3000 francs, but in time the demand grew so great that recourse was had not only to goat- and horse-hair, but to less pleasant sources of supply. Thus Samuel Pepys tells us that in 1665 he refrained from wearing

a new periwig lest the hair had been cut off the heads of people dead of the plague. The grey powdered wig belongs to the eighteenth century, and is not found before 1700.[1] The lace collar, now that it was entirely concealed by hair falling in long locks on to shoulders and back, assumed a new cut. After the fifties appeared a collar which was narrower round the neck but came well down in front. This was the *cravate*, said to have derived its name from a regiment of Croatians enlisted since 1636 in the service of the French crown.[2] Blount gives

PORTRAIT OF A LADY
Rembrandt. 1639
*Photo F. Bruckmann A.-G., Munich*

the earliest description of this new collar in 1656,[3] and an example of it may be seen in Rembrandt's famous *Syndics of the Drapers' Guild*, painted in 1661 (see p. 174). On October 19, 1662, Samuel Pepys put on his first new lace band, for which he had paid £3. This was cheap at the price, for Charles II gave £20 and James II from £29 to £36 for theirs.

The riding-boot with wide top filled in with lace (see p. 87),

---

[1] Powdered hair was known in France a hundred years earlier than this, and again in about 1630, but the fashion was only temporary.

[2] The author is confusing the 'cravat' (see, for example, pp. 192, 197, 200, 203) with its predecessor, the 'falling band' (see pp. 174, 177-181). *Cravate* is an old form of *croate* (Croat). The *cravate* emulated the neckband worn by the regiment in question.

[3] Thomas Blount, *Glossographia* (1656): "*Crabbat* (Fr.), . . . a new fashioned Gorget which women wear."

which fashion actually countenanced in the drawing-room, made way in time for the shoe. In 1660 one Nicolas Lestrange, a shoemaker at Bordeaux, presented Louis XIV as a wedding gift with a pair of shoes of his own making. They had broad vamps and high red heels, and were trimmed over the instep with bows sixteen inches in span adorned at the ends with smaller bows having rosette centres. The King was enchanted with the model, showered all manner of favours upon the designer, and declared that in future he would always wear shoes of this shape (see pp. 169, 171, 172). Picture for a moment the appearance of a gentleman in the young days of Louis XIV, in a jacket inadequate to cover a shirt that bulges on all sides, in petticoats instead of breeches, with his person covered in lace trimming and ribbon bows, a lace collar, lace frills dropping over his hands and the calves of his legs, a blond wig, and over-stockings [1] falling untidily over

ELIZABETH JACOBSZ BAS
Rembrandt. C. 1642
*Photo F. Bruckmann A.-G., Munich*

an under-pair (see p. 135), and you will agree with Quicherat's comment that this was a strangely effeminate guise for a generation perpetually involved in war.[2] In point of fact, warlike times were responsible for the simplification of masculine costume. General Tilly's coat (see p. 73) was one example of a cut adapted to practical requirements, and just as the rhinegrave, a garment originally worn by Dutch peasants [?], took the world of fashion by storm, so that German peasant coat, penetrating by way of the army into wider spheres, was not a mere temporary whim of fashion, but became in time an accepted style. The wars which kept Germany, England, and France in arms for so many decades

[1] 'Boot-hose.'
[2] J. Quicherat, *Histoire du costume en France* (1875), p. 516.

made it a physical necessity for the participants to don a dress very different in style from the effeminate get-up of the beaux. The reaction against the petticoat finery of the gentlemen set in at the very moment when extravagance and display in dress were at their height. It started, in England, as an expression of political and religious conviction, and caused the dress and demeanour of Roundheads and Cavaliers to differ as widely as did their views. The Puritans, no less

AN ENGLISHWOMAN IN SPRING
COSTUME
Wenzel Hollar. 1644

disgusted at the frivolity of court morals than at the arbitrary measures of the Government, in order to distinguish themselves from their hated monarch with his sycophants and courtiers, dressed as simply and unobtrusively as possible. Their garments were dingy and homely, sometimes even deliberately careless in appearance. Sir Philip Warwick remembered seeing Cromwell in 1640 in soiled linen with a blood-flecked collar, and in a suit that might have been made by an inferior village tailor. As the Cavaliers wore their hair in carefully dressed curls the Puritans cut theirs short. Mrs Lucy Hutchinson, in the memoir of her husband,[1] tells us that "Among other affected habits" of these Puritans they often cut their hair "close round their heads . . . as was something ridiculous to behold" and earned them the scornful term of Roundhead. This simplicity lasted as long as the party found itself in opposition, but when Cromwell became Lord Protector he and his family and adherents adopted court clothing. At the first audience of the Spanish ambassador Harrison, Cromwell's adjutant, appeared in a scarlet dress smothered in ribbons and lace. Samuel Pepys, who was brought up on strictly Puritanical lines, tells us that on July 10, 1660, he put on a silk suit for the first time in his

[1] *Memoirs of the Life of Colonel Hutchinson* (first edition, 1806).

146

life. Then, however, vanity ran away with him on seven-league boots, and we hear much of purchases of costly suits, laces, and perukes.

In France every one followed the lead of the handsome, charming young King. Louis XIV never descended to the level of creating fashions, he left that to lesser lights. The first of these to set the tone was M. de Montauron, a wealthy financier; after his ruin his place was filled by the Duc de Candale and after him by M. Langlée, a person of dubious descent and still more doubtful means of existence, but who managed to find favour at court. His business it was to create the fashions, but fashionable wear followed the King's choice. Louis spent long and frequent periods with his army in order that the fame of his generals' victories and conquests might reflect on him. He always went with a large suite, which did not lack ladies, each of whom, according to the account of the Savoy ambassador, the Marquis de St Maurice, took with her

AN ENGLISHWOMAN IN
WINTER COSTUME
Wenzel Hollar. 1644

at least five or six dresses worth £30 to £40 apiece. But it was not meet that the King should go otherwise clad than his soldiers, and so the military coat, retained by Louis XIV when he returned to court from the field, became a garment of distinction. One of the chief changes in its cut is attributed to the King; when the court went into mourning in 1665 for his father-in-law, King Philip IV of Spain, Louis announced that when the period of mourning was over he intended to discard the slit sleeve which permitted the entire length of the shirt sleeve to show. Thereafter sleeves were seamed up (see pp. 200, 205, 208, 213, 214), and at about the same time the coat started to display the slightly fashioned waist retained for so many years. By about 1680 the coat had become the most important article of masculine attire, a *rôle* that it has not lost. It reached to the knees, covering not only the breeches but the *veste*,[1] a development of the doublet (see pp. 197, 200); the breeches, indeed, now that the long stocking reached over the knee, were completely hidden. But if the man's suit was now less complicated it was no plainer. The coat, it is true, was worn closed, but it offered ample space for trimmings, while the sleeves, turned back in wide cuffs to the elbow, left room below for lace frills (see pp. 197, 200). Although trimming with embroideries was

A LADY IN A 'MILLSTONE' RUFF
Wenzel Hollar. 1645

A BOURGEOIS WOMAN OF ANTWERP
Wenzel Hollar. 1643

prohibited in France, the King, by establishing in 1664 the *justaucorps à brevet*,[2] reserved to himself and his favourites the privilege to wear them. The holder of this *brevet* enjoyed the right to wear a blue coat lined with red and embroidered throughout in silver and gold, and the garment entitled him to accompany the King wherever he went without special invitation. As the number of such privileged persons was very restricted—it is said, to sixty—a French courtier cherished henceforth no dearer ambition than inclusion among these chosen few. "Ludicrous though it may seem," says August von Heyden, "similar honours would be courted with equal ardour to-day." [3] In this way embroidering could be driven to extravagant lengths. The coat worn for his marriage by the Prince de Conti is described by Mme de Sévigné as a

---

[1] The forerunner of the modern waistcoat.
[2] Literally, 'close coat permitted by royal warrant.'
[3] In his *Trachtenkunde* (1889), p. 207.

straw-coloured brocade patterned in black velvet thickly encrusted in diamonds, and one of the sights of the Duc de Bourgogne's wedding was the gentlemen in their gold brocade coats embroidered in gold. Broad ribbon bows now took the place of the narrow loops and were used for fastening the cravat at the neck (see pp. 197, 200, 203); knots of ribbon also hung from one shoulder (see p. 200). About 1690 they went out of fashion, but the lace cravat and cuffs remained (see p. 208); according to *Le Mercure de France* of 1681, a

AN ANTWERP LADY OF
QUALITY
Wenzel Hollar. 1647

THE WIFE OF THE LORD
MAYOR OF LONDON
Wenzel Hollar. 1646

gentleman's lace set could be had from fifty louis-d'or.[1] An anecdote told in 1690 by the Marquis de Dangeau shows that even officers in the field could not dispense with lace. According to this story, the officers of the French army besieged by the Spanish, having come to an end of their lace, requested the Spanish general, the Marquis de Castañaga, to let some lace-dealers through so that they might replenish their stocks. This he agreed to at once, and the French selected lace to the value of some ten thousand crowns.[2] But when they attempted to pay the dealers refused the money, saying that the order had been given by the general.

In the early part of the century men wore quantities of jewels (see p. 52). Hans Meinhard von Schönberg, who died

---

[1] Valued at 10 livres when first coined in 1640, it reached a value of 40 livres under Louis XV.

[2] The silver crown (*écus d'argent*) was worth 60 sols or sous, the livre (or franc) 20 sous.

in 1616, left jewellery to the value of several thousand thalers, and Katharina von Canstein's family album shows not only **Jewellery** young bloods but sixty-year-olds like von Hanxleben, Chamberlain of Paderborn Cathedral, in bracelets. The great Sully wore bracelets until his dying day in 1641, and we are justified in picturing Shakespeare in bracelets and earrings. When Endymion Porter[1] joined the English Embassy in Madrid he wore his wife's diamond necklace as a hatband. Marmaduke Rawdon, a London

FUR AND BROCADE MUFF
Wenzel Hollar. 1647

merchant, affected an emerald hatband, and when the Governor of Virginia, Yardley, commissioned his friend Susan Moseley in 1620 to buy him a hatband at The Hague he empowered her to spend 1000 ducats. Later, however, rings, chains, bracelets, and hatbands vanished from the attire of the man of fashion, chains being reserved as an insignia of municipal office, diamond ornaments for great State occasions. Louis XIV was adorned with brilliants to the value of 14,000,000 francs when he received the Turkish ambassador in 1669, and the buttons used to trim the suit of gold fabric of the Emperor Leopold on the occasion of his marriage to the Infanta Margaret Theresa[2] each consisted of nine large diamonds.

[1] 1587–1649; English royalist, employed as envoy to Spain to negotiate peace.
[2] See p. 94.

THE BALL

Miniature by Abraham Bosse

*Kaiser Friedrich Museum, Berlin*

150

THE ARRIVAL OF THE DUTCH AMBASSADOR AT MÜNSTER

Gerard Ter Borch

*Photo F. Bruckmann A.-G., Munich*

When fashions became modelled on those of the French court feminine costume, which under Dutch influence had Ladies'<br>Dress<br>late in the<br>Century become far simpler, verged once more toward luxury and display. The chief change lay in the bold adoption of low necks (see pp. 182, 190, 191, 194), for tulle palatines [1] and wide lace collars were now out of vogue. In 1660 Lady Lambert purchased seven lace collars at £50 apiece for which a year or so later she had no further use. Neck and bosom were now left undraped, and the opening of the dress was edged with only a narrow lace. The sleeve, however, made up for this paucity of trimming, for the narrow elbow-sleeve finished in a becoming billow of wide lace (see p. 197). The waist-line, pushed down by the deep *décolleté*, ended in front in an elongated point, and the skirt, which toward the fifties fell freely, at most opening in front in a narrow ∧, was now raised to give full effect to the underskirt. It was caught in ample folds to the back, where it fell in a long train (see p. 160). The idea of a visible underskirt was repeated in the bodice, which parted to display a triangular front of other material, over which it was held with laces and clasps (see p. 209). Since for convenience sake this triangular front was made as a separate part and just slipped in, as it still is to-day in certain national costumes, it was known as a *Stecker*.[2] The feminine fashion of low necks which we find in the seventeenth century, which from modest beginnings with transparent veiling ended in a flagrant *décolleté*, was not maintained without considerable opposition. Moralists and satirists vied with each other in denouncing the style, and incidentally provoked the local authorities to strong measures. In 1634 and 1637 and again in 1640 Leipzig prohibited "bodices cut so low as to leave neck and bosom scandalously, impudently, and offensively bare," and in 1662 the Brunswick town council forbade

---

[1] Called after Charlotte of the Palatinate ("Liselotte"), who strove to induce greater modesty in dress by wearing a gauze wrap over her fashionable low bodice. John Evelyn, in his *Fop Dictionary* (in *Mundus Muliebris*, 1690), describes the winter palatine as "Formerly call'd Sables, or Tippet, because made of the Tails of that Animal."

[2] Actually, a stomacher. *Stecken* may mean 'to stick or pin in.'

women and girls to appear "with their figures shamefully and scandalously exposed and with a mere pretence at veiling in the shape of thin, transparent crape." Louis XIII, so the story runs, once spat a mouthful of wine into the immodestly low front of a lady's dress. This vulgar prank proved no more

ANTONIO ALVAREZ D'AVILA
Pierre Simon

successful in modifying the *décolleté* of French ladies of fashion than did magisterial decrees in stopping the mode, and by the end of the century the high-necked dress was a thing of the past. Even Spanish women, who were little influenced by French styles, adopted low necks of a cut peculiar to themselves. A woman with a well-developed figure was regarded with shocked eyes in Spain, and so from early youth every effort was made to retard its growth. Quite small girls had to wear sheets of lead on their breasts, thus acquiring concavities in place of graceful swellings. So, as Spanish ladies had nothing worth attention in front, they wore their dresses low at the back, and one can picture the horror of an elegant French dame like Mme de Motteville when, at the meeting of the French and Spanish courts in 1660, she espied the garb of her foreign sisters. Louis XIV, upon

A SCHOLAR AND HIS WIFE
Gonzalez Cocques

seeing his youthful bride in her dreadful Spanish attire, merely confessed to Marshal Turenne and the Prince de Conti to some disappointment at her want of attraction, but John Evelyn, on May 30, 1662, went so far as to describe the appearance of Charles II's Queen and her Portuguese maids of honour as "monstrous."

As it was usual for both skirts of the dress to show, and a train falls all the better for being heavy, fashion decreed silk and velvet for the upper (caught-up) skirt and rich trimmings and embroidery for underskirt and bodice. Since whole garments of cloth-of-gold or -silver could only be afforded by the few—by princes, or by people like M. Langlée who kept themselves by gambling—these materials were usually reserved for the stomacher. Mme de Sévigné wrote her daughter a glowing account of an attention paid by Langlée to Mme de Montespan. He bribed her tailor to make an irreparable misfit of a dress she had ordered for a great court occasion, and when the lady abandoned herself to the expected frenzy of despair he had her presented with another perfectly fitting dress of gold material thickly embroidered in different shades

COMPANY
Pieter de Hooch

of gold—in the words of this delightful correspondent, "the most heavenly stuff imaginable." That such heavy garments cannot have made for comfort is shown by the remark, in 1679, of Sophia, Electress of Hanover, that the French Queen had difficulty in moving about, as the embroidery on her dress made it heavier than a horse's trappings; the wedding-dress of Princess Dorothea Sophia of Brandenburg in 1701, which weighed a hundredweight, must, says one Herr von Besser, have been somewhat tiring. The introduction of black lace in France in 1660 made lace more fashionable than ever, and whole dresses were now made of it. Mme de Sévigné writes in 1676 most approvingly of such *robes transparentes*,[1]

[1] They were frequently made of painted gauze.

which were worn over underdresses of gold or silver brocade, and Samuel Pepys, in 1666, is loud in his praises of Mrs Stewart, whom he saw "in black and white lace." When a certain Herr Leo, in the capacity of tutor, accompanied young Herr von Lüttichau in 1672 on a grand tour his letters from Paris and Saumur to Frau von Schleinitz, an aunt of his pupil, amounted to fashion articles. "The bodice or corslet," he wrote,

PORTRAIT OF A LADY
Wenzel Hollar. 1648

may consist of white, brown, or other taffeta embroidered in black, brown, or coloured flowers. With a white or silvery skirt a white bodice worked in black looks very dignified and well. Underskirts are covered, crosswise or lengthwise, in bands of lace.

Another time he mentions scarlet petticoats covered in white lace. In this century scarlet and brick-red played almost as great a part as black (see plates facing pp. 106, 136, 150). Even with black clothing both ladies and gentlemen wore trimmings of scarlet ribbon (see plate facing p. 198), and sometimes they dressed themselves and their offspring in flaming red. When Winthrop, Governor of Massachusetts,[1] placed a large order for cloth in England in 1633 he got only red cloth, for his agent could procure no other.

Apart from heavy silks and brocades there were lighter fabrics, a silk-and-wool mixture called camlet,[2] a silk-and-cotton one known as ferrandine or bombasine; *Tobien* was the name in Germany for a moire taffeta, *Karteck* for a thin silk used for lining. A thin grey silk-and-cotton material known in France as *grisette* and favoured by women of the poorer classes ultimately surrendered its name to the

**Names**

---

[1] John Winthrop (1588–1649), first Governor of Massachusetts.
[2] In the latter part of the century, according to Quicherat (*Histoire du costume en France*), French camlet ceased to contain silk.

MARIE-LOUISE DE TASSIS
Anthony Van Dyck
*Liechtenstein Gallery, Vienna*

156

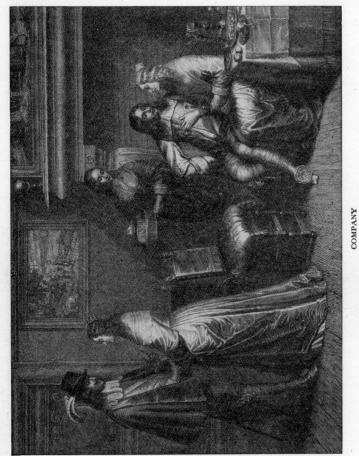

**COMPANY**

Scheltius van Bolswert, after Christoffel van der Laemen

lower ranks of ladies of easy virtue. The extravagant fantasy still exhibited by Parisian textile dealers at the end of the eighteenth century in the names they invented for fashionable shades was already visible in the early seventeenth. Agrippa d'Aubigné [1] records "nun's belly," "merry widow," "sick Spaniard," "gibbering ape," "constipation," "smallpox," and other such witty names for certain ranges of yellow, green, and grey. The French, with their subtle instinct for fashion and her follies, did not content themselves with a careful nomenclature for materials and colours, but assigned to every trifle of wear a special name and meaning. Gentlemen's fal-lals were briefly summed up as the *petite-oie*,[2] but for ladies a careful distinction was drawn between the knot over the brow—the *fripon* ('rogue'), that at the waist—the *badin* ('rascal'), and the breast-knot— the *tâtez-y* ('touch and see'). The favour worn over the heart was called the *mignon* ('pet'), that at the neck the *assassin* ('assassin'),

A LADY IN A LONG CAP
Wenzel Hollar. 1648

that on the head the *galant* ('lover'), while those concealed in more private places went by the name of *nonpareilles* ('incomparables'). The *culbute* ('head-over-heels') was the name for the bow worn at the back of the coif, the *effrontée* ('hussy') for the coiffure with the hair strained back to show the ears, which features, on ladies, it had kept concealed for many years.

About 1640 the popular style of feminine hairdressing was a parting across the front of the head and a fringe of loose

**Ladies' Coiffure** tendrils (see pp. 92, 111, 113, 115, 117, 132, 133, and plate facing p. 76). This fringe, which resembled the *Simpelfransen* ('simpleton fringe') of some fifty

---

[1] Theodore-Agrippa d'Aubigné, grandfather of Mme de Maintenon and author of the satirical *Aventures du baron de Faeneste* from which these names are quoted.
[2] See p. 142, *n*. 4.

158

years back in Germany, was called in France *garcettes*.[1] In the fifties and sixties the long ringlets on either side of the face were raised to form tight bunches over the ears, while a couple of corkscrew curls also hung down the back (see pp. 182, 190, 191, and plate facing p. 176). In 1671 a Paris *coiffeuse* originated a new style of hairdressing by disposing of the corkscrew curls and setting the hair in loose (but close) curls all round the head—the *chou frisè* ('savoy cabbage') coiffure known as *hurluberlu* [2] (see p. 193, and plate facing p. 192). Mme de Sévigné, who describes it in detail but not very clearly, in a letter of April 4 of this year to her daughter, the Comtesse de Grignan, could not find a good word to say of the new style at first, but the sight of the Duchesse de Sully and the Comtesse de Guiche with their hair

A PORTRAIT
Gortzius Geldorp

dressed in this way promptly dispelled her disapproval, and she urged her daughter to follow their example. Ladies' heads used to be further adorned with a feast—often a surfeit—of flowers, and Ninon de Lenclos once likened Mme de Choiseul's head to "spring-time in a country inn." [3] When fashion decreed a train to the dress the tendency to add to feminine stature also affected the coiffure, for the hair was dressed higher and higher on the head, and instead of a low forehead partly

[1] From the Spanish *garceta*, 'a heron'; also, through comparison with the heron's aigrette, 'fringe.' *Cf.* the English fringe of that time and the American 'bang.'

[2] Origin uncertain. The word is used in France in the sense of 'a harum-scarum.'

[3] Apparently an allusion to the bad paintings of the four seasons found in most country inns at that date.

concealed by ringlets a high, often a shaved one, was now the mode. And when the desired effect surpassed the powers of real or even of artificial hair the aid of ribbons and lace was invoked (see pp. 204, 207). Thus was produced the The famous fontange [1] described by Saint-Simon, La Fontange Bédollière, Regnard, and others, which remained in fashion until after the death of Louis XIV (see pp. 206,

A FAMILY GROUP
Barend Graat. 1657

209, 216). Bussy Rabutin [2] is the authority for attributing this headdress to one of the King's mistresses, the Duchesse de Fontange. "A stupid creature, but good-hearted and as lovely as an angel," is how Liselotte describes her. In point of fact, she died at the age of twenty in 1681, whereas the erection named after her did not make its appearance until 1684. It survived for some thirty years, as even Louis XIV,

[1] Antoine Furetière, in his *Dictionnaire universel* (1727), describes it then as a knot of ribbon worn on the front of the hair. It was equally applied to the high wired cap, also called a *commode* or tower (see pp. 206, 209).
[2] Roger de Rabutin, Count de Bussy (1618–93).

A Portrait
Franz Hals
*Kaiser Friedrich Museum, Berlin*                    160

who was soon sick of the sight of such a coiffure, could not persuade the ladies of his court to discard it. It was as violently denounced as *décolleté* had been. Friedrich Lucae, pastor of Rothenburg-in-Hesse, who had already achieved distinction by spreading his handkerchief over the low neck of a communicant, also declared his attitude to the new style of hairdressing by snatching the fontange from the head of a lady as he passed her in the street.

Although the linen of both sexes rivalled in costliness the material and the trimming of their *Under-linen* dresses, such extravagance by no means went hand in hand with cleanliness. That washing was considered unhealthy is proved by some French daily rules of 1640, which run, "An occasional bath should be taken, the hands washed daily, and the face every day or so." In 1670 Antoine de Courtin goes so far as to advise bathing the feet. Such lack of hygiene explains the prodigal use of strong scents. According to Mme de Motteville, Marion de l'Orme spent 50,000 francs a year—of her lover's money—on perfumes. "He stinks like a corpse," so the Marquise de Verneuil, mistress of Henry IV of France, is reported to have said of her royal lord, and Mme de Motteville, again, tells us that the hands of Queen Christina of Sweden (see above), so famous for their beauty, could not be seen for dirt. "French ladies," wrote A. Leo to Frau von Schleinitz, "are very particular about their dresses to make up for their frequently unwashed bodies and chemises." On sending his fair correspondent a packet of soap from Italy this gentleman thought fit to enclose detailed directions for its

QUEEN CHRISTINA OF SWEDEN
Robert Nanteuil

use. If Scarron[1] was right in asserting that it was customary to change one's body linen only once a month, then the well-worn tale of the Infanta Isabella Clara Eugenia's chemise loses much of its point. In 1601, so this story runs, when

QUEEN MARIA ANNA OF SPAIN
Velazquez. 1658
*Photo F. Bruckmann A.-G., Munich*

her consort opened siege on Ostend, the Infanta swore not to change her chemise until he had taken the city. Bound by this oath, she was forced to wear the garment from June 12, 1601, until September 22, 1604, and her once white-linen was "Isabel-coloured" when she took it off. If underwear, though costly, was seldom clean this was partly due to the materials used in its make. Queen Marie de Médicis wore red silk chemises trimmed with gold embroidery and linen ones worked in gold, and Chancellor von Beichling used night apparel of brocade. In 1660 Lady Lambert paid £300 for half a dozen lace-trimmed chemises. Both ladies and gentlemen spent large sums on lace handkerchiefs—the Venetian agent Paolo di Sera asked the Grand Duke of Tuscany 200 ducats for one—but for practical purposes they made use of their fingers and

[1] Paul Scarron (1610-60), French writer and the first husband of Mme de Maintenon.

THE PARABLE OF DIVES AND LAZARUS

Abraham Bosse

the floor. Since personal linen was dear and not often changed large stocks were not necessary. In Vienna it was customary for the bride to present the bridegroom as his wedding gift with linen consisting of half a dozen shirts, handkerchiefs, collars, and cuffs. Henry IV of France boasted a dozen shirts and four handkerchiefs, most of them torn, and the wardrobe of the Earl of Rutland, in 1612, contained nineteen lace-trimmed and twenty-one plain shirts—for those days a magnificent supply. Samuel Pepys tells us that at one time Charles II had only two handkerchiefs and three shirts to his name,[1] while Moncada and Osorio, two Spanish authors of this century, maintained that there were at least three million Spaniards without a shirt to their backs. It is somewhat surprising, therefore, to find Guarinonius,[2] in the early days of the century, groaning over the "awful washing-days" in his home. The Archduchess of Tirol had all her fine washing sent to Florentine nunneries instead of having it done in Innsbruck, and it was quite usual for Parisians to pack their dirty linen off to Holland to be made clean. Let those who wear *Röllchen*[3] take comfort in the thought that, according to the washing lists preserved in the Germanische Museum at Nuremberg and the Ferdinandeum at Innsbruck, gentlemen, even in these early days, also wore detachable cuffs, and that this despised article can therefore boast quite a considerable ancestry.

The development of costume during the seventeenth century endowed the lives of the cultured nations of Europe with
French a new interest in the shape of fashion. Even before
Modes this century the main lines governing the contour of the human figure had followed certain common laws; in the fifteenth century the Burgundian, in the sixteenth the Spanish court had exercised a decisive influence over style in dress. The existence of a general likeness, however, did not

[1] The author has apparently the following passage in mind: "The King having at this day no handkerchers, and but three bands to his neck" (*Diary*, September 2, 1667). But the Officer of the Wardrobe tells Pepys that "it is the grooms taking away the King's linen at the quarter's end, as their fees, which makes this great want."
[2] Hippolytus Guarinonius of Halle (1571–1654), doctor and writer.
[3] The name for the detachable cuffs worn in Germany in recent times.

obliterate a number of distinctive features in cut, and until
well into the seventeenth century it is always possible to
distinguish persons of different countries, towns, and ranks.

THE INFANTA MARIA THERESA
Velazquez. 1659

In *The Seven Deadly Sinnes of London*, by Thomas Dekker (1606),
we read:

For an English-mans suite is like a traitors bodie that hath
beene hanged, drawne, and quartered, and is set up in severall
places: the collor of his Duble in France: the wing and narrow sleeve in Italy: the short waste hangs over a Dutch Botchers
stall in Utrich: his huge sloppes speakes Spanish: Polonia
gives him the Bootes: And thus we that mocke everie Nation,
for keeping one fashion, yet steale patches from everie one of

them, to peece out our pride, are now laughing-stocks to them, because their cut so scurvily becomes us.

But things soon changed, and in the thirties, in the upper strata of society, began that striving after harmony in dress which we name the birth of fashion. In Germany the new styles were due as much to the belligerent conditions of those

A DUTCH COUPLE
Bartholomeus van der Helst

decades as to the mingling of the various features of dress of the different towns and provinces. But the noteworthy point is that upon the majority of Louis XIV the French court assumed the lead in all matters of dress, and French modes became then international modes. The styles worn at the court of Louis XIV were followed by all and sundry; gradually they were emulated by every cultured nation and rank, and national and individual distinctions in dress vanished. Hottenroth[1] draws a witty comparison between the power of fashion and the infectious act of yawning; it was, indeed, true that a fashion had only to declare itself for all European nations simultaneously to catch the infection. Turn to German satirists of that time such as Logau, Moscherosch, Ellinger, Lauremberg, Rachel, and Weise, and the stigma of aping the French model appears to have attached to Germany alone. Then examine the literature of England and Holland: parallel phenomena are found. Moreover, new fashions were greeted, even in Paris, with such jeers and raising of eyebrows that it is difficult to credit this city with

[1] In his *Handbuch der deutschen Tracht* (1891–92).

A PORTRAIT

Gerard Ter Borch.  1642
*Alte Pinakothek, Munich*

166

being their birthplace. None could account for the strange new spirit or explain the lightning change not only in fashions but in manners and modes of thought. When the early decades of the seventeenth century ushered in a new conception of modes the word *Mode* was used for the first time in Germany in the present-day sense. From the French expression *à la mode* German writers coined the word *alamodisch*, and

GEERTRUIDA DEN DUBBELDE
Bartholomeus van der Helst

expended their entire wit on this score on the imaginary person of Herr Alamodo, upon whom between 1625 and 1630 a veritable hailstorm of satires and caricatures was rained. That foreign fashions would necessarily be accompanied by foreign customs and foreign crimes was the idea underlying most of the ditties and lampoons, such as the *Kartell stuzerischen Aufzugs* (*Society for Foppish Dress*), the *Alamodische Kleiderteuffel* (*Fashionable Dress Fiend*), the *Alamodische Hobelbank* (*Fashionable Carpenter's Bench*), the *Alamodische Sittenschul* (*School of Fashionable Morals*), and so on, which poked fun at fashionable folk.

> In *à la mode* rig-out
> Thoughts *à la mode* begin;
> For as you change without,
> So do you change within,

runs a rhyme by Friedrich von Logau. The essential difference between the French modes of this date and their predecessors was the frequent changes they imposed on their apostles. "Collars change nearly as often as the moon's phases," complains Harsdörffer,[1] and Moscherosch has some bitter words to say concerning the manifold styles of foreign

ANNA MARIA PELLER
Bartholomäus Kilian

hat adopted by novelty-seekers. "Now a hat like a buttercrock, now one like a sugar-loaf, now one like a biretta, now a yard-wide sombrero; then hats of goat-hair, camel-hair, beaver-hair, monkey-hair, fool's hair; a hat like a Black Forest cheese, another like a Dutch cheese, another like a Münster cheese." In 1649 Gabriel Naudé [2] too derided the perpetually changing headgear of French modes. "One man," he writes, "dons a sugar-loaf hat pointed like a pyramid, so that it dances about on his periwig as he walks; another must have his flat, with a cord round, *à la mauvais*

---

[1] Georg Philipp Harsdörffer (1607–58), founder of the literary society of the Pegnitzschäfer (see p. 40).
[2] In his *Mascurat*.

*garçon*,[1] laden with plumage to stop it from blowing away."
In 1641 Hans Georg von dem Borne, Chancellor of the

LOUIS XIV RECEIVING AN ADDRESS ON HIS ENTRY INTO PARIS, 1660
François Chauveau

Neumark, complained to the Elector of Brandenburg that
fashions changed once a month and that each new style was
as ridiculous and fantastic as the last. When the Electress

[1] *I.e.*, with a cocked brim.

Palatine, in 1650, displayed her ample wardrobe with pride to her sister-in-law Sophia, the latter vented considerable scorn on the subject. It was no longer the fashion to have so many clothes at once, she said; one ought always to be getting new ones. When Margaret of Navarre, once the acknowledged queen of fashion and *bon ton*, returned to Paris in 1606 after a prolonged absence she was held up as a laughing-stock and parodied in a ballet as a comic type of bygone days. Fashion in Paris now was set by the pretty milliners. "No one dresses so charmingly as the assistants in the fashion shops of the Palais-Royal" (see p. 109), writes Fitelieu in 1642,[1] and a Leipzig sumptuary law of 1640 regrets to state "that certain womenfolk are making a regular business of designing new styles and models of dresses and footwear." But apparently municipal interference was not of much use, for in the following year a Dr Höppner was suing a tailor "for attracting large crowds of women and girls by advertising new fashions for sale."

Sumptuary laws, which were already following hard on one another in the latter part of the sixteenth century when Sumptuary fashions were set by Spain, swelled in the seven-Laws teenth to a positive flood. Whether in Virginia, Massachusetts, Germany, Spain, England, or France—everywhere it was the same story, and the verdict passed by the Burgomaster of Berlin on the Berlin sumptuary law of 1604— "It had no effect and did no good"—was universally true. In Germany these laws aimed not only at controlling fashions and stemming extravagance, but at retaining visible class distinctions. Thus in 1626 the Elector Maximilian of Bavaria divided his subjects into peasantry, lesser *bourgeoisie*, industry and trade, chancery officials and clerks, patriciate, knights and nobles, doctors and licentiates, counts and barons, and fixed with the utmost precision the dress and trimmings of each of these classes. The Duke of Gotha went to work on similar lines with the six classes in which he placed his subjects in 1695, and Nuremberg, Stralsund, Danzig, Stettin, Lübeck, and Leipzig showed no less zeal in "announcing what each

[1] In his *Contre-mode*.

THE MEETING OF LOUIS XIV AND PHILIP IV ON THE ISLAND OF PHEASANTS
Edme Jeaurat. 1660

class might and might not wear." The stuffs, furs, laces, and trimming permitted to each class were minutely prescribed

LOUIS XIV VISITING THE OBSERVATORY
Sébastien Leclerc

in true and irritating bureaucratic style, and the advent of each new fashion was followed by the "most noble, wise, and prudent authorities" with the issue of prohibitions. In

172

A PORTRAIT

Gerard Ter Borch. 1642

*Alte Pinakothek, Munich*

1662 Dresden banned periwigs and Brunswick ribbon trimmings, in 1680 Leipzig prohibited trains. And with what result? To answer this we need only turn back to the Nuremberg sumptuary law of 1657, which runs:

> It is unfortunately an established fact that both men- and womenfolk have, in utterly irresponsible manner, driven extravagance in dress and new styles to such shameful and wanton extremes that the different classes are barely to be known apart.

"Display in dress has reached such a pitch," writes Hans Georg von dem Borne as early as 1641, "that it is impossible to distinguish artisan from nobleman or nobleman from prince." This was a particularly sore point with the nobility, who, not content to leave it to their features to reveal their rank, felt constrained to show it in their dress. The levelling tendency apparently frightened them more than the threat:

PORTRAIT OF A LADY
Franz Hals

> God, the Almighty Creator and Preserver of all mankind, Who has often, for their vainglory, committed whole towns and countries to destruction, will, unless the Paternal decree is forthwith obeyed, also find cause to punish this place.

But although the many penalties inflicted show in what bitter earnest these innumerable laws were contrived, not one of them could be enforced. At Leipzig in 1618 Dr Jonas Möstel, son of the burgomaster, was fined 1000 thalers for wearing black velvet on his wedding day; at Dresden in 1628 Maria Hendschel had to pay the penalty of venturing to don a velvet cap and fur-trimmed cloak; and at Nuremberg in 1661 the printer Christoph Endter, as a result not only of dressing his wife too grandly but of giving his dog a silver collar, was subjected to repeated fines. Since vanity, as we know, makes it impossible for the fair sex ever to regard unmoved the finery of others, it is probable that feminine jealousy kept a watchful eye on all fine feathers and induced the authorities to punish crimes which they might otherwise have winked at. Report ran that Peter Glitze, the school-director of Meissen, might never have ascended the scaffold had not his

THE SYNDICS OF THE DRAPERS' GUILD
Rembrandt. 1661

wife incurred the implacable enmity of a Dresden lady of rank by snatching from under her very eyes at the annual fair a costly coif of the latest style. Nevertheless the *bourgeois* continued to purchase sables, the worker to don sword and spurs; no embargo on foreign goods could check, even for a moment, the victorious march of French modes. A contemporary estimate of Johann Becher [1] puts Germany's annual consumption of French luxury goods, in those early days, at four million thalers, and Bolingbroke valued English imports of French millinery during the reign of Charles II at some eleven million francs a year [*sic*]. At Chemnitz in 1629 Philipp Hainhofer notes in his diary, "The women here are

[1] Johann Joachim Becher (1635–82), German chemist and scholar, promoted schemes for manufacture and trade in cloth and silk.

fine and stylish"; elsewhere he says, "In Saxony the women dress wonderfully well; even the old ones are as fine as can be, some of them looking, in their caps, like old jades in new hames." At Ancona in 1688 Misson remarks, "The Ladies

THE DUKE OF ORLEANS AT A TILT DRESSED AS A PERSIAN KING
François Chauveau. 1662

of Quality imitate in their Dress the French Fashion, but after so aukward a Manner, that they appear more ridiculous than the others in their own Country Dress." [1] Considerations of good taste, economy, or patriotism, it seems, were no more capable than sumptuary laws of quelling French modes. "I must tell you," writes Liselotte in 1695, "that Germans are

[1] *Misson's Travels.*

more than ever intent on fashion." In 1666 Charles II took
steps to free himself and his court from the tyranny of French
dress. How he did this we learn from both John Evelyn and
Samuel Pepys. On October 8 the King "in Council declared
his resolution of setting a fashion for clothes, which he will
never alter." [1] He carried this out for the first time on the

BARONESS AMALIE VON STUBENBERG
Bartholomäus Kilian. 1661

15th, appearing in "a comely vest, after the Persian mode," [2]
"and a coat over it, and the legs ruffled with black riband
like a pigeon's leg, . . . a very fine and handsome garment." [3]
But already on the 30th we hear that it was "too good to
hold," [4] and this is the last mention both of this habit and
of the new fashion for the ladies at court of which Lady
Carteret expressed her dislike.[5] At the close of the seventeenth

[1] Pepys, *Diary*, October 8, 1666.     [2] Evelyn, *Diary*, October 18, 1666.
[3] Pepys, *Diary*, October 15, 1666.     [4] Evelyn, *Diary*, October 30, 1666.
[5] "To wear short coats above their ancles."—Pepys, *loc. cit.*

A Nobleman and his Wife

Abraham van den Tempel

*Kaiser Friedrich Museum, Berlin*

176

century French fashions were everywhere in high society
holding undisputed sway, and from there filtered slowly but
steadily down the scale. When Louis XIV occupied Strassburg in 1681 its inhabitants were ordered to discard German

**LOUIS XIV**
Antoine Masson, after Charles Le Brun

costume and within four months to assume French attire.
Such drastic action was really superfluous, for in the other
Imperial cities newfangled modes were already beginning to
oust traditional styles, or at least to push them into the background, whence they only emerged as ceremonial garments,

M³                         177

for use on such solemn occasions as weddings, baptisms, and the like.

Of all the new fancies of fashion not one was so vigorously championed as the periwig. The fashion of natural long hair

LOUIS XIV,
Robert Nanteuil. 1663.

had already provoked the authorities to repressive measures, which grew even more severe when, in the natural course of events, the new style of hairdressing was followed by new styles of moustache and beard. "Proper thieves' hair," Moscherosch calls these falling locks, and says that they were

178

PORTRAIT OF A GENTLEMAN
Gerard Ter Borch

"contrived by foreign rogues, to conceal the fact that they had had an ear lopped for some misdeed." But gallants were very proud of them; in 1624 one Thomas Schlegel was run through by a nobleman simply for daring to wear long hair, like a lord. When the periwig advanced from a necessary evil to an indispensable fashion there arose a perfect storm of abuse. In a violent diatribe against the employment of false

hair, issued in 1642 under the *nom de plume* of Irenäus Poimenander, Pastor Gottfried Uden reminded the pious of the story of Absalom. The strife provoked by his treatise was aggravated by the interference of experts from various learned faculties. It assumed an increasingly theological—that is to say, unreasonable — character, and calm was only restored when Claude de Saumaise,[1] in the name of common sense, pointed out the triviality of the point under dispute. The German

GUILLAUME DE BRISACIER
Antoine Masson, after Pierre Mignard. 1664

clergy, however, refrained from wearing wigs, and in Saxony, for instance, spurned the fashion until it was expressly sanctioned in 1692 by the provincial diet. Then, indeed, these appointed representatives of prejudice and superstition proceeded to cling assiduously to the wig long after it had gone out of fashion.

In Venice, whose aristocracy were great sticklers for convention, the periwig also proved a subject of friction. The first person to appear in the Square of St Mark in a peruke was Scipione Collalto, who brought it from France in 1668. The State inquisitors, fearful of all innovations, prohibited its wear, a prohibition which held good until their successors

[1] See p. 191.

A DANCING PARTY (PART)
In the manner of Gonzalez Cocques
*Museum of Art and Industry, Berlin*

came into office and sanctioned the small wig called the *calotta*. Niccolo Erizzo left a clause in his will disinheriting his son in favour of the Hospital of the Pietà should he persist in wearing a periwig—which he did! Another enemy of this

JOHANN LEONHARD SCHORER
Bartholomäus Kilian, after Franz Friedrich
Franck. 1665

innovation, Antonio Correr, assembled a company of two hundred and fifty gentlemen, all of whom swore to abjure the wig. How many of this company remained true to their vow history does not record, only that the founder himself died in 1757 in the full glory of his own locks. But ever since the day when the Doge Giovanni Cornaro opened the Venice Grand Council in a wig its opponents were fighting a losing fight.

# CHAPTER IV
## SOCIAL LIFE

Iɴ this century of chronic war fever manners and social conventions were martial and rough, and remained even in the best circles indescribably coarse. The Duc Manners d'Épernon and Marshal de Vitry once administered a hiding to Archbishop Sourdis of Bordeaux, the Duke

PORTRAIT
Caspar Netscher. 1668

of Orleans actually boxed Richelieu's ears in the Cardinal's own palace, and husbands of princely rank, like the Electors Charles Louis of the Palatinate and George Louis of Hanover, thought nothing of settling marital disputes by cuffing their consorts at table.

Certain surviving court ordinances of this period afford delightful glimpses of the habits of the upper classes. The table regulations of one of the Austrian archdukes for the year 1624 admonish gentlemen to come sober and decently dressed to table, and to refrain from sucking their fingers, using the tablecloth as a handkerchief, or spitting into their plates. At the same date we find the Dukes of Pomerania and Mecklen-

PORTRAIT
Cesar van Everdingen. 1671
*Photo F. Bruckmann A.-G., Munich*

burg trying to control the uproar at meals, forbidding gentlemen to throw nibbled bones and crockery at each other or "absent-mindedly" to slip their napkins into their pockets. When pages became obstreperous the chamberlain would bring them to their senses by administering correction in person.

The chief recreation then of the gilded youth of London consisted in making themselves a nightly danger in the streets, attacking coaches and sedan-chairs, mauling the bearers and footboys, and terrifying the ladies. Brawling and vulgar horseplay were the order of the day at German universities.

Friedrich Lucae tells us that in the year 1662 a Heidelberg student, out of sheer bravado, ate in the dissecting-room a pound of flesh cut from the body of a gallows victim. No less delightful, apparently, were the pleasures of tender youth. In Holland Pastor Hartmann saw children catching dogs and beating them to death with sticks, to the great entertainment of adult onlookers. That the tormenting of animals was a

sanctioned pastime for the young is evident from the many contemporary pictures showing boys amusing themselves with captive birds; there is Rubens' painting of his son, for instance, or that in which Murillo actually depicts the Christ-child playing with a "fowl of the air." Of the brutality and depravity prevalent in Germany during and after the Thirty Years War Moscherosch in his *Gesichte*,[1] as well as Grimmelshausen[2] in his *Simplicissimus* and in his *Landstörtzerin Courasche*, has drawn some gruesome pictures.

MARIA MARTHA BESSERER (1634–72)
Joachim von Sandrart

Such brutality and licence could only be outgrown by the establishment of some moral code capable of bridling men's passions and teaching them altruism. This code was supplied by etiquette, the rules of which the seventeenth century developed into a positive science. The institution of etiquette was an attempt to eliminate, with the aid of a strict code of mutual obligations, that egotistical attitude to life where self counted for everything and one's neighbour for nothing, and where only rights but no duties were recognized.

Etiquette

Incidentally, also, this important step created such sparring and wrangling that questions of priority and etiquette gradu-

[1] See p. 140, *n.* 1.
[2] J. J. Christoffel von Grimmelshausen, *c.* 1621–76.

PAINTER AND MODEL
Louis Le Nain
*Alte Pinakothek, Munich*

ally overshadowed all others, and the theological points
hitherto contested with so much passion vanished into thin
air. The Peace of Westphalia was imperilled because Sweden
and France could not agree on their respective order of
precedence, so the French went to Münster, the Swedes to
Osnabrück, to frame the treaty. "The next delicate and
knotty points involved,"
says Gottfried Stieve,
a contemporary writer,
"concerned the signing of
the treaty, for the parties
could not agree on the
manner or order in which
his Imperial Roman
Majesty and the other
rulers should sign." And
so things went on, and
the long-drawn-out peace
negotiations were almost
entirely taken up with
disputes over competence
and precedence, a state
of affairs which also
applied to the perma-
nent Diet at Ratisbon. A
great part of the letters
and memoirs of Sophia,

FASHIONABLE FOLK
Romeyn de Hooghe

Electress of Hanover,[1] is concerned with news of the
honours accorded her and the titles conferred on her lord.
When this gifted lady journeyed to France in 1679 to visit
her sister at Maubuisson and her niece Liselotte in Paris
she had need of all the diplomacy at her command to hold
her own on such points as refusing a tabouret[2] or paying
the proper compliments. That a matter like etiquette should
have caused the seventeenth and even the eighteenth century

[1] See p. 91, n. 2.
[2] In France certain persons had a right to a seat on a small stool in the
queen's presence.

such brain-racking and trouble seems ludicrous to-day, but we must remember that to the society of those times a transition stage of punctiliousness furnished the essential step toward greater social freedom and ease. France was no less pettily punctilious in such matters than Germany. "The etiquette here is quite nauseating," wrote Liselotte once from Paris, and Mme de Motteville, in her memoirs, tells us that the subjects of vital interest at the French court were who might

and might not sit in the presence of the Queen, who had the right to an armchair, who only to a tabouret, who might drive in a coach to the Louvre, and so on. Disputes about precedence or about priority of place for carriages sometimes ended in bloodshed. During the Ratisbon Diet of 1622 a scuffle took place in the Imperial chapel between Count Onate, the Spanish Ambassador, and Gritti, the Venetian Legate, because neither gentleman would make way for the other; and a similar situation at the Maundy Thursday procession in Vienna in 1655 resulted in the Mantuan and Genoese Legates

A GENTLEMAN IN A
RHINEGRAVE
Sébastien Leclerc

belabouring each other with their wax torches. Even in Rome it was found necessary to suspend the religious processions for a time, as the various brotherhoods taking part could not agree on their order, and on every occasion there was trouble. The Marquis de St Maurice relates how at the great court festivals and theatrical entertainments in France it was quite usual for some of the male guests to attack each other with sticks and have to be separated by the soldiery. The Saxon Electorate decided in 1680 that, in order to avoid disputes, persons having an entry at court should be divided, in order of rank, into fifty-two classes —a number ultimately reduced to thirty-two. Titles and appellations—things of no small moment—soon became more long-winded than ever, and special study was needed to master the rules that governed them. Nuremberg families entitled to a seat in the municipality, for instance, whose appellation had hitherto been "noble, perpetual, and gentle," in 1687 suddenly demanded the addition of "most" before "gentle." Families not so entitled, who so far had contented themselves with "honourable and perpetual," now claimed to be styled "most gentle and gracious." Ladies of quality, accustomed until the early days of the seventeenth century to be addressed as "most honourable and virtuous," now wished to be called "high- and well-born," while unmarried girls of a certain rank, who until 1600 had simply been "maid," then became "miss"— an appellation soon to become so general that it was bestowed on young ladies of noble as well as of princely rank.

FASHIONABLE FOLK
Romeyn de Hooghe

Until midway through the century gentlemen had always kept on their hats, even when they entered a room in which ladies were present, though to be permitted to retain a hat in the presence of the king was a jealously guarded right of ambassadors. In 1615 Count Christoph von Dohna claimed the privilege, as envoy of the Evangelical Union, of appearing with covered head before Marie de Médicis; upon meeting with a refusal he preferred to depart without fulfilling his mission rather than lower his prestige. But with the change in social conventions came a change in manners, and gentlemen now removed their hats in greeting. Hitherto they had given greeting by tilting their hats back without actually baring their heads, but the new custom was to remove the hat with a flourish, the better to display its feather trimming. As clothing became more comfortable movements became freer. "Good heavens!" cries Moscherosch:

What a foolish foreign gait, what an extraordinary manner and mien! That is hopping and skipping, not walking! Why

FASHIONABLE FOLK
Romeyn de Hooghe

do you make movements with your hands like a conjurer? Why such bowing and scraping, such twisting and turning? You look for all the world like a pocket-knife going snap!

The new manners scandalized a good many people; both Spanish and French passed remarks in Paris on the extraordinary politeness of Louis XIII, and Frederick of the Palatinate ('the Winter King') got a 'bad name' in Prague for his genteel manners. "He makes himself cheap with people," was the verdict; "he takes off his hat to all and sundry." Not until the latter part of the century, when the

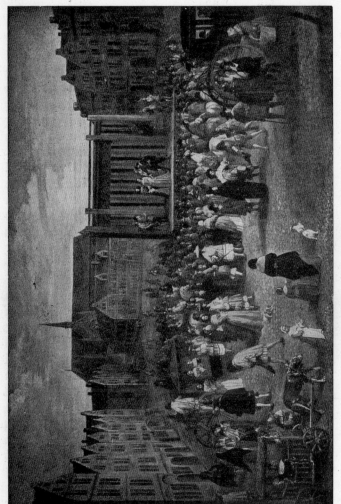

AN OPEN-AIR THEATRE IN THE MARKET-SQUARE

Adam van der Meulen

example was set by Louis XIV, were good manners esteemed. The Duc de Saint-Simon and Liselotte are unanimous in their praise of this king, especially of his faultless courtesy to women of all ranks.

That social intercourse and relations between the sexes became, during the seventeenth century, both more agreeable and more graceful was due to the influence acquired during the course of this century by women. Frenchwomen were the first to require a display of intellect and wit on the part of the gentlemen who courted their favour, and the drawing-room was the place in which women first laid claim to equality with the stronger sex by pitting against man's crude strength the finer weapons of the intellect. As early as 1616 the German traveller Jodokus Zinzerling recorded his admiration of the liveliness and grace of Frenchwomen, who could chatter away with the greatest ease on the toughest themes. In the *salon* to which Catherine de Vivonne, Marquise de Rambouillet, and her daughter Julie d'Angennes, Duchesse de Montausier, attracted the intellects of French society social intercourse was raised to the level of an art, and toward the middle of the century the Hôtel de Rambouillet was a famous centre of culture. The ideal fostered here, of a social life governed by æsthetic principles, was gradually emulated elsewhere, and similar *salons* were formed by Mme de Sévigné, Mme de la Fayette, the Duchesses

Salons

MME DE SÉVIGNÉ
Nicolas Édelinck

de Longueville, d'Hautefort, and de Chevreuse, the Princesse de Bourbon-Condé, the Grande Mademoiselle,[1] and other ladies of the high aristocracy. These highbrow circles are described in the novels of Calprenède,[2] de Gomberville,[3] Honoré d'Urfé,[4] Mme de la Fayette,[5] and, last but not least, of Mlle de Scudéry.[6] The *Artamène* and *Clélie* of the last-named furnish a complete picture of life in high society, for they show

MME DE MONTESPAN
Gérard Édelinck

how worthless its refinements became when the wealthy *bourgeois* started to ape them. Studied manners and flowery speech then became mere affectations, and while Chapelle and Bachaumont,[7] Saumaise,[8] Saint-Évremond,[9] and others have made merry with their pens over the provincial pedantry of these people, Molière in his *Précieuses ridicules* has held them up as a laughing-stock for all time. In England the Countess of Derby, the Countess of Bedford, and others presided over *salons*; in Holland the house of the learned Anna Maria van Schurmann (see p. 136) was a meeting-place of the *intelligentsia*; while in Rome Maria Mancini-Colonna and her sister, Hortense Mancini-Mazarin, made a brief endeavour to form a *coterie* on similar lines.

[1] Anne-Marie-Louise d'Orléans, Duchesse de Montpensier (1627–93), niece of Louis XIII.
[2] Gautier de Costes de la Calprenède (*c.* 1610–63), writer of romances and plays.
[3] Marin-Leroy de Gomberville (1600–74), poet and writer of romances.
[4] 1568–1625, writer of romances.
[5] Marie de la Vergne, Comtesse de la Fayette (1634–93), woman of letters.
[6] Madelène de Scudéry (1607–1701), leader of a literary *salon*.
[7] Claude-Luillier Chapelle (1626–86) and François de Bachaumont (1624–1702) are known for their joint work, *Voyage en Provence*.
[8] Claude de Saumaise (1588–1653).
[9] Charles de Saint-Évremond (1610–1703).

In Germany a suitable centre was lacking, and except for the somewhat pedantic attempt of Georg Philipp Harsdörffer at Nuremberg in 1644 no such circles existed. Harsdörffer organized a social attraction which he describes as "conversation-games for ladies [*sic*] which may, in honourable and virtuous society, supply a popular means of combining instruction with diversion." He shows us Angelica von Keuschewitz, a young lady of rank, Raymund Discretin, a travelled and erudite youth, Julia von Freudenstein, a gifted matron, Vespasian von Lustgau, an aged courtier, Cassandra Schönlebin, another young lady of rank, and Degenwert von Ruhmeck, a shrewd and able soldier, indulging in this pastime, and also tells us how he set about raising the tone of society. The men had to organize games of forfeits the redemption of which involved quickness and wit.

THE EARL OF SANDWICH
Abraham Bloteling, after Sir Peter Lely

For instance, the offender had to play the fool for the whole evening or tell stories in words lacking a given letter or make verses rhyming with a given syllable; or else he must tell nothing but untruths, whereupon he would immediately overwhelm the company with compliments. The party had also to amuse themselves by making anagrams—live, evil, vile, veil— or tax their ingenuity in finding replies to such questions as, Should one aspire to know what others know or what they do not know? The eight bulky volumes of this guide to diversion, the contents of which Harsdörffer has culled from French and Italian sources, smack considerably of pedantry, but their aim —to replace the customary pleasures of the table by more elevated forms of entertainment—is deserving of praise. Harsdörffer himself calls toping "a laudable weakness," thereby

PRINCESS MARIA MANCINI-COLONNA
Pierre Mignard
*Kaiser Friedrich Museum, Berlin*

voicing the opinion of his contemporaries, who regarded it as a necessary, even an essential, failing. "We Germans," writes Professor Wagenseil, the great scholar,[1] in 1686, "are one and all slaves to the shameful Drinking vice of drunkenness." A more than true verdict, for it was considered hygienic in Germany to get drunk at least once a fortnight. When Misson noted at Nuremberg in 1687, "Where drinking is concerned the habits of the Germans are hopeless," he was by no means exaggerating.

The great lords were the first to set a bad example. When Christian II, Elector of Saxony, was leaving Prague in 1610 he thanked the Emperor for "entertaining him so well that he had never known a sober moment." In much the same words had the Duke of Holstein expressed his gratitude for

MAGDALENA SIBYLLE OF WÜRTTEMBERG
Bartholomäus Kilian

the fine carousals prepared for him in 1604 by Duke Francis of Pomerania. The more drink a man could stand the greater his name. The Imperial Vice-Chancellor, Peter Heinrich von Strahlendorff, who died in 1637, was one of the heaviest drinkers of his day, outdone only, perhaps, by the Brandenburg Chamberlain, Kurt von Burgsdorf, who could dispose of eighteen measures of wine at a time. Of Count Jakob Fugger, the head of his great house, Elias Holl asserts that "he drank himself full after every midday meal," and an incident at the court of Stuttgart in 1651 described by Sophia, Electress of Hanover, is quite characteristic of the times. In a drinking match organized by the gentlemen the Duke of

[1] Johann Christoph Wagenseil (1633–1705).

Holstein, so the Electress relates, toasted her in such a bumper glass that he returned its entire content forthwith; nothing daunted, however, he refilled the glass and drank her health anew. Count Christoph von Dohna was present at Heidelberg at a drinking-bout where Frederick, Count Palatine, and the Margrave of Baden became so merry that they cut the beards off their inebriated guests with their own hands, "which sadly

MAKING MUSIC
Adriaen Hanneman
*Photo F. Bruckmann A.-G., Munich*

damaged the appearance of the old privy councillors, who were scarcely recognizable."

There was nothing to choose between the classes. While the Prince-Bishop of Speyer complained that the Catholic priests were always tippling Pastor Saubert, of Nuremberg, recorded in his diary in 1646 that the Lutheran clergy had been unable to take the early service because they had not properly slept off their last night's carousal. This fondness for the bottle accounts for the custom of presenting silver goblets as testimonials or keepsakes. Friedrich Lucae kept a careful account of all such gifts, and the famous Jena theologian Johann Gerhard received as many as sixty-eight in his life. A poor drinker ran great risks. In 1641 Councillor von Zastrow was stabbed by a fellow-toper because he was too fuddled to return a toast; at a breakfast at the Count Palatine's house, during the Nuremberg Diet of 1611, when all

DRAWING BY ADAM VAN DER MEULEN
*Print Room of the Berlin Museums*

the company were 'as drunk as lords,' Count von Dohna, in order to avoid any further toasting, feigned sleep; and Philipp Hainhofer, who had no head for drink, was once at Stettin obliged to appeal to the Duke not to let too much liquor be pressed upon him. In 1613, when he attended the nuptials of the Duchess Magdalen with Count Palatine von Neuburg, Hainhofer recorded the marvellous fact that he "had not seen a single tipsy person the whole week." The need in Germany for temperance societies was recognized by Maurice, Landgrave of Hesse, who founded one in 1601, and by Jakob Balde, the Jesuit, who organized at Munich a Congregation Macilentorum (Society of the Lean); but their results are not recorded. It would nevertheless be grossly unfair to assume that only German men were over-addicted to the bottle. Things were no different in England and

A PARISIAN COUPLE
Sébastien Leclerc. 1679

France, which accounts for the English custom, dating from this time, for ladies to rise first from the table and leave the gentlemen to their drink.

People of those days were also prodigious eaters, and must have had truly enviable stomachs. Philipp Hainhofer was **Eating** entertained in 1617 by the *Kantor* [1] at Stettin to a meal which started at ten A.M. and lasted till six P.M.; and in 1610 Guarinonius tells us that a middle-class banquet in Germany usually consisted of six courses, each composed of nine different dishes, and that while noble houses only offered their guests three courses each course comprised a hundred dishes. From the collection of menus

[1] *Kantor* in Prussia often denoted one who held a position in the Church as well as in a school.

A PARISIAN FASHION SHOP
Jean Bérain. 1678

of the court of Hanover made by Malortie[1] we learn that on Sunday, June 13, 1647, the first course was two kinds of wine soup, rib of venison, roast game, carp, pasties, stuffed breast of lamb, ham of wild boar, roast veal, turkey, pullet, beef, and crucian. The second course was roast lamb, fig tart, fritters, pike, venison, artichokes, beef and dumplings, veal, baked pickled beef, crab, sucking-pig, calves' tripe, and neats' feet. Then followed dessert. The French kings are said to have been particularly heavy eaters. Henry IV was continually suffering from a surfeit of melon, and Liselotte saw Louis XIV consume a meal consisting of four plates of soup, a whole pheasant, a partridge, a plateful of salad and one of Irish stew, two thick slices of ham, a helping of pea-hen, sweetmeats, and fruit. Food then was flavoured with strong spices to an extent that would not appeal to the modern palate. "Our food to-day," groaned Moscherosch once, "comes not from the kitchen but from the apothecary's shop." Table decoration took the form of show-dishes "destined to render the banquet famous and give the guests food for thought." At Munich in 1613 we hear of a moving figure of Fortune and a Pegasus releasing the Pierian spring —masterpieces of the pastry-cook Michael Lochmaier, of Donauwörth. In this year, too, the Elector of Cologne spent 11,000 thalers on appointments for a banquet he intended to give the princes attending the Ratisbon Diet. But, alas, the plague came, and the banquet failed to take place. At a feast in Hanover given by Count Königsmarck the table was graced by a huge basket containing a laying hen, whose eggs, when opened, revealed roasted ortolans, while from the basket poured a bevy of dancing children. The next course was a pie from which live birds took wing, and there were further wonderful dishes.

Table manners were simple in the extreme. Liquid foods were drunk with a spoon from a common dish; solids were eaten, as best might be, with the fingers. Montaigne once complained that he ate so quickly he was always biting his fingers, and we know that Anne of Austria and Louis XIV,

[1] C. Ernst von Malortie, *Das Menu* (1882).

PORTRAIT OF A LADY
Unknown master
*Von Lipperheide Library of Costume, Berlin*

for example, always ate in this way. Georges Calviac, the traveller, noticed that in Germany and Italy in 1650 every guest was given a knife, but that in France a whole party had to make shift with two or three between them. Forks in their early days were used only for serving. Thomas Coryate, the English traveller, was amazed to see people in Italy in 1608 doing a thing "not used in any other country

A PARISIAN COUPLE
Sébastien Leclerc. 1679

that I saw in my travels"[1]—holding meat on their plate with a fork and cutting it with a knife, and was equally astonished to find that one gave considerable offence by eating or helping oneself with one's fingers. But when he tried to introduce this remarkable new custom into England he was merely ridiculed and nicknamed "Furcifer."[2] The fork did not come into general use until midway through the century. We still find Moscherosch referring to "the foolishness of eating salad with a fork" as "a trick savouring of foreign ill-breeding." The fashion of changing the plates for every course was initiated at the Hôtel de Rambouillet, and

[1] Thomas Coryate, *Crudities* (1611).
[2] Yoke-bearer, gallows-rogue (*furca*, 'fork' + *fero*, 'bear'). The *furca* was an instrument of punishment in the shape of a fork: a yoke.

199

the Duc de Montausier is credited with having introduced serving-spoons, for before his day the server always helped the guests with his own spoon. The only concession to cleanliness then was the washing of hands before and after meals, the handing of a towel to distinguished guests being a jealously guarded privilege.

Gentlemen were expected to include carving among their

PARISIAN FASHION-PLATES
Bonnart. 1680

accomplishments. Carving was a highly important art, the subject of special instruction and of quite an extensive literature. A man of parts must also be able to fold a serviette neatly and skilfully into the form of a cabbage, a clerical collar, a biretta, a turban, a valance, and so on, and to cut apples and pears into such fancy shapes as a heart, a fool's head, or a Spanish [sic] cross.[1] Herr von Vieregg, Chamber-

[1] The second edition (1666) of *L'Escole parfaite des officiers de bouche* (1662), a book of cookery and table management, contains diagrams for cutting apples and other dessert fruits into fancy shapes; one of the shapes for apples is a Lorraine cross.

lain at the electoral court of Cologne and Bavaria, owed his ennoblement solely to the skill with which he wielded the carving-knife. One of the favourite diversions at the German dinner-table was the composing of impromptu doggerel. When liver was included on the menu it was passed round on the spit and each guest had to compose a rhyme on it.[1] There were books giving guidance in this art.

PARISIAN FASHION-PLATES
Bonnart. 1683

The seventeenth-century contributions to the pleasures of the table include the fruit-ice (an Italian concoction), iced lemonade, and liqueurs—either introduced into Paris or invented by Procope Cutelli[2]—and sparkling wines—produced by Dom Perignon, cellarer at the Benedictine Abbey of Hautvillier. In this century, too, the three beverages—tea, coffee, and chocolate—without which not the most modest household could be imagined to-day came into more general

[1] The German word for doggerel is *Leberreim* ('liver-rhyme').
[2] A well-known Parisian *limonadier*.

use. Chocolate was imported into Spain from Mexico in 1520, but did not reach England until 1657 and France until 1661. China tea was brought to Europe by the Jesuits;

FREDERICK WILLIAM OF BRANDENBURG, THE GREAT ELECTOR
Antoine Masson. 1683

from 1638 it was procurable from Russia, later from Holland.[1] Its price was so exorbitant at first that the English East India Company when it presented the Queen of England in 1664

[1] Although the Portuguese have claimed priority in the matter, the credit for introducing China tea to Europe is usually given to the Dutch East India Company. According to *Meyers Konversations-Lexikon*, China tea reached Paris in 1635, Russia in 1638, and England in 1650.

with two pounds of tea was making her a munificent gift.
Cardinal Mazarin and Chancellor Séguier were instrumental
in popularizing tea in France, while its reception in Holland

MAX EMMANUEL, ELECTOR OF BAVARIA
Karl von Amling. 1687

was so enthusiastic as to cause Bontekoe, the well-known
physician, to declare that good health was entirely dependent
upon drinking two or three hundred cups of tea a day. Coffee
was a Turkish product, and was traded for the first time at
Marseilles in 1650; not until 1655, however, did the taste
for it begin to spread slowly in France, and as late as Ledieu's

time[1] we find this *abbé* marvelling to see a cup of coffee being served after dinner to every guest at Fénelon's parties.[2] Germany acquired a taste for coffee after the famous siege of Vienna by the Turks and established its first coffee-house in 1683, Nuremberg and Ratisbon following suit in 1686, Hamburg in 1687. The opening of coffee-houses in London gave quite new colour to the life of the capital, for they became the gathering-places of its masculine society, which flocked there to smoke.

PARISIAN FASHION-PLATE
Bonnart

Europe [Germany ?] is indebted to England and Holland jointly for the introduction of a new comfort in life in the shape of tobacco. Holland was acquainted with the practice of smoking by 1580, England possibly some ten years earlier.[3] The German traveller Paul Hentzner, who between 1596 and 1600 accompanied a Herr von Rehdiger, of Breslau, on a grand tour, mentions "tobacco-drinking," and in 1629 Hainhofer discusses with friends "the German tobacco-tippling," and cannot understand "this English fashion of taking it." Smoking was violently attacked

**Tobacco**

[1] Francois Ledieu (*d.* 1713), secretary to Bossuet.
[2] *Meyers Konversations-Lexikon* gives 1671 and 1672 as the dates of the first coffee-houses at Marseilles and Paris respectively.
[3] Tobacco-smoking, according to *Meyers Konversations-Lexikon*, was introduced into Spain from the West Indies in the middle of the sixteenth century, and into England from Virginia in 1586. English and Dutch troops brought the custom to Germany in 1622, during the Thirty Years War.

at first. The pedantic James I of England actually wrote a book against tobacco,[1] and spoke of it as "the lively image and pattern of hell." Penalties attended its use, which in Berlin was still punishable in 1675 by imprisonment and the pillory. In 1616 'tobacco-drinker' was a term of affront in France, but in 1644 the French started to grow tobacco, and when, in 1674, the State established a sale monopoly opinion veered round, for the proceeds from taxation had risen in twenty years from 150,000 livres to 4,000,000. Although smoking was considered ungenteel in France, snuff-taking found devotees galore, even at court, notwithstanding Louis XIV's dislike of it. "It infuriates me," wrote Liselotte, "to see all the womenfolk here with dirty noses." In America tobacco, as well as being a creature comfort, was

PARISIAN FASHION-PLATE
Bonnart

employed as a medium of payment; Noah Rogers, a tailor of Lancaster, received eighty pounds of tobacco in 1643 for a man's dress and sixty pounds in 1690 for a lady's.

Seventeenth-century folk had few distractions; in middle-class houses these were practically confined to the great family occasions of baptism, marriage, and interment, Diversions upon which, therefore, no time or expense was spared. Probably the annual fairs provided the greatest diversion, and even Henry IV of France and Marie de Médicis looked forward all the year to the Saint-Germain

[1] *A Counterblaste to Tobacco* (1604).

Fair. They offered so much to tempt the eye and the purse. One of the sights in 1606 was Apollonia Schreier, a young woman who had subsisted for five years without food or drink; in 1614 there was Eva Vliege, a virgin whose sole nourishment for seventeen years had consisted of the perfume of flowers. From 1617 the Colloredo brothers—Siamese twins—were on show for money for a whole generation; and in 1624 the Leipzig Fair boasted a lucky-pot containing prizes

LADIES WEARING THE FONTANGE
Sébastien Leclerc

to the value of 17,000 gulden. A parallel with the rhymester, who visited middle-class houses on festive occasions to sing the praises of the family and provide entertainment, was furnished by the court fool, who was still an indispensable adjunct. At all the courts Hainhofer attended "the buffoons provided interludes at table." We hear of Marie de Médicis borrowing the Duc de Lorraine's court fool, and has not Velazquez immortalized the dreadful company of dwarfs, half-wits, and deformities who adorned the court of Madrid in the capacity of jesters? The great court festivals cost a mint of money. The wedding of the Duke of Württemberg with a Brandenburg princess in 1609 cost 800,000 gulden; one of the many festivities organized by the Duc de Vendôme

PORTRAIT OF A LADY
Flemish master
*Art Gallery, Schleissheim*

at Anet ran away with 100,000 livres; and the entertainment offered to Louis XIV at Chantilly in 1671 by Condé cost the great man not only a million francs, but his *maître-d'hôtel* as well. Mme de Sévigné tells the story of how the famous Vatel completely lost his nerve on this occasion and fell on his sword because he feared that the salt-water fish intended

IN THE BOUDOIR
J.-Dieu de Saint-Jean

for the King's table would not arrive in time. Court entertainments, notwithstanding their magnitude and splendour—on February 2, 1693, at Hanover, for instance, a court dinner was followed by a masked ball given by the Countess Hohenlohe, and that by a French comedy, supper, and a ball—do not seem to have provided unfailing diversion. Under Marie de Médicis court festivities were notorious for their appalling confusion and disorder. As late as 1679 the Electress Sophia writes from Versailles, "The entertainments at the French court are so packed and stifling they are nothing but a misery," and in 1698 we find Liselotte lamenting [at Port-Royal], "This is the dullest place in the world." Hunting as a pastime was chiefly confined to the wholesale slaughtering of beaten-up animals in the castle grounds or game-parks, and was, like the animal-baiting then so popular, a brutal and cowardly sport. In Berlin in 1614 Count von Dohna attended a bear-baiting; at Innsbruck in 1628 Hainhofer saw "a lioness and a magnificent tiger cast to the bulls"; and in London both Zinzerling and Hentzner [1] witnessed fights between dogs, bears, and bulls.

Balls in the seventeenth century were very different from those held to-day. Gentlemen did not seek their own partners: the master of the ceremonies arranged the couples, and only one couple danced at a time. Nor were the character and time of the dances anything like our modern ones. The saraband was proud and majestic, the chaconne must be footed with measured tread; the musette demanded a pastoral grace, the siciliana a light step, the jig a merry hop, and so on. The slow, solemn rhythm of most of the dancing gave the famous Mattheson [2] the idea of turning some of the best-known chorales into dance-music. This he did by retaining the melodies just as they were and simply

**Dances**

PARISIAN FASHION-PLATE
Bonnart

[1] See p. 204.
[2] Johann Mattheson (1681–1764), German composer.

changing the time. So *Wenn wir in höchsten Nöten sind* (*When in the Hour of Utmost Need*) became a minuet; *Wie schön leuchtet der Morgenstern* (*O Morning Star, how Fair and Bright*) a gavotte, *Herr Jesus Christ, Du höchstes Gut* (*Lord Jesu Christ, Pure Source of All*) a saraband, *Werde munter, mein Gemüte* (*Sink not yet, my Soul, to Slumber*)

PARISIAN FASHION-PLATE
Bonnart

a *bourrée*. The dancing couples could not let themselves go; they had to apply themselves and do their best, for they were the cynosure of all eyes. Louis XIV took daily dancing lessons for twenty years. When the minuet, the first musical setting of which we owe to Lully, became fashionable in 1663 it was voted the king of dances; it required three months of preliminary training. August Bohse-Talander,[1] by the way, once advised the middle classes not to dance too well lest they arouse the hatred and jealousy of the nobility. Among the most passionate devotees of dancing were Sully, who even in his old age amused himself every evening by dancing a *pas seul* embellished by capers of his own devising, and Cardinal Richelieu, who notwithstanding his rank danced a saraband before Anne of Austria attired in green velvet breeches, with bells on his feet and castanets. The first real social dance was the courant with twelve couples, a favourite dance of Louis XIV, and the first dance in which more than one couple might take the floor

---

[1] 1661–1740, German jurist and novelist; his real surname was Bohse, Talander his literary pseudonym.

together was the so-called *rigaudon de la paix*, borrowed by France from England.[1]

Not even Beauchamps' and Lully's[2] most seductive compositions, however, could keep society from abandoning an innocent pleasure for the more thrilling pastime of **Gambling** gambling. Liselotte wrote in 1695 from Paris:

Dancing is now quite out of fashion—at every party here people play *lansquenet*;[3] they play for outrageously high stakes and act as if demented, screaming, banging on the table so that the whole room shakes, uttering blasphemies that make one's blood run cold, behaving, in short, as if they had lost their senses.

EZECHIEL VON SPANHEIM
Pieter van Gunst

This Palatine princess who gives such a graphic description of gambling took no interest in it herself and had once to suffer the reproach, "There is nothing to be done with you since you don't gamble." High stakes and cheating were the order of the day, for it was considered quite the thing for ladies and gentlemen to supplement their incomes in this way. When Mme de Motteville saw Mazarin for the last time she found the dying Cardinal busy weighing gold pieces and setting aside the light ones for play. The great weaknesses of Henry IV of France were women and gambling, in which latter sport his consort Marie de Médicis bid fair to rival her lord. While Marshal d'Estrées once lost 100,000 livres

[1] Grove's *Dictionary of Music* (1928) says that the rigadoon probably came from France, though its popularity in England has caused some writers to place its origin there. Danced in France in the time of Louis XIII, it was not popular in England until the end of the seventeenth century.

[2] Beauchamps (*d.* 1695), the dancing-master of Louis XIV, arranged the court ballets, while Jean-Baptiste Lully (1633–87) was his director of music.

[3] A French corruption of the German *Landsknecht* ('mercenary'); a game of hazard with cards.

in an evening and the Abbé de Gordes won 150,000 from Louis XIV at a sitting, Ernest, Duke of Hanover, was gallant enough to let the lovely Maria Mancini-Colonna win 30,000 thalers from him in this way. Her still more beautiful sister, Hortense Mancini-Mazarin, after a highly chequered career, retained

FRANÇOIS MANSART, THE ARCHITECT
Gérard Édelinck

only two passions in life—gambling and drink. Gambling was rife at the Imperial court and in Vienna society. In 1696 the Austrian envoy, the Prince de Ligne (see p. 213), lost 50,000 gulden in play to Count Hallweil, the Chamberlain, and rid himself of his debt by inveigling his creditor for a walk, killing him in a wood, and hiding the body.

Roads were so bad and unsafe and vehicles so poor that

travelling in the seventeenth century was anything but a pleasure. "To-morrow is a good day to travel, the day after still better. If you stay here, I will," were the words read by Pastor Hartmann on the walls of an inn outside the gates of Hamburg. The so-called 'gentleman's tour' [1] completed the schooling of a young man of good

**Travel**

ANNE-MARIE-LOUISE DE MÉDICIS IN HUNTING
COSTUME
Jan van Douven

family. He would, often when still in his teens, set out with a tutor to visit foreign courts and universities, a visit to Italy being still regarded during the early part of the century as an indispensable adjunct to education. Visitors to the churches of San Domenico in Siena and San Antonio in Padua will find there even to-day numbers of memorials to young Germans who succumbed to fever or duelling on one of these tours. "To see everything of note in Rome one must get hold of a good antiquarian," says Misson. But not every visitor there could count on so worthy a relative as Fabian Konopacki, Chamberlain at the court of Clement VII. This good uncle of the Counts von Dohna made his nephews' stay in the Eternal City pleasant in every way, and even procured them music lessons with the famous Nanini. [2] Later the grand tour ceased to include Italy, for, in the words of Gottfried Stieve, "Because no gentleman's education was considered

---

[1] Usually called the Grand Tour.
[2] Giovanni Maria Nanini (1540–1607), composer.

UNKNOWN PRINCESSES OF THE HOUSE OF
HABSBURG
Miniatures

*National Museum of Bavaria, Munich*

complete unless he had studied deportment and languages in France for a while—no matter if he had traversed the whole wide world besides—so it became almost a necessary evil to spend some time in this country." Horseback was the only means of travel, for even better carriages than were available then could never have negotiated such bad roads. The first coaches were built in Italy, and in 1599 Marshal Bassompierre brought to Paris the first coach with glass windows. The windows must have been the only recommendation of these vehicles, for far greater attention was paid to luxurious fittings than to making them comfortable. The wedding carriage in which the Infanta Margaret entered Vienna cost 100,000 thalers, and that of the Princess Henrietta, who married Duke Rudolph Augustus of Hanover in 1668, 20,000 thalers. In 1681 another Hanoverian

THE PRINCE DE LIGNE, PORTUGUESE
AMBASSADOR IN VIENNA
Peter Schenck

ruler—Duke Ernest Augustus—owned fifty all-gilt six-horse coaches. The first comfortable conveyance was constructed in 1660 in Berlin; of light build and with only two seats, the 'berlin' remained a popular vehicle of travel for nearly two centuries. So appalling were the roads along which the unwieldy coaches had to struggle that in 1664 the ladies-in-waiting accompanying the Electress Sophia of Hanover to Florence were overturned nine times in one day; so they decided to make the return journey to Modena straight away on foot. In 1657 Pastor Hartmann took six days to get from Berlin to Stettin, and in 1687 Misson spent just as long on the way between Heidelberg and Nuremberg, and had to pay 30 thalers for the ride. Until

LOUIS XIV
Antoine Masson. 1697

midway through the century the post, the management of which in Germany was a privilege of the Taxis family,[1]

[1] This noble German house, more rightly styled 'von Thurn und Taxis,' had for many years inherited the office of Postmaster-General.

AN INN PARLOUR ABOUT 1640
From a student's album

carried only letters and packets; then the administration established a service of stage-coaches which carried passengers from Frankfort-on-the-Main at stated intervals to Paris in six days and to Madrid in fifteen. The stage-coach which plied regularly between London and Oxford took two days; that between London and York in the winter six days. When the London-to-Oxford 'flying coach' accomplished its journey (now just over an hour by rail) in only thirteen hours it was regarded as a marvel of speed. In districts far removed

DRAWING BY SÉBASTIEN LECLERC

from traffic routes travelling was dependent upon chance opportunities. Friedrich Lucae had intended to pass six months at Frankfort-on-the-Oder in order to attend the university, but no sooner had he arrived than off he went again, for "God decreed otherwise," he writes, "by ordaining that an empty stage-coach should be returning to Brieg." The roads were not only bad, but so unsafe that even the Empress, travelling once with a big retinue to a spa, was waylaid and robbed. This was the age of highwaymen and cut-throats, out for booty on land and water alike. Dutch pirates scoured the Rhine right up to Andernach; freebooters from Tunis, Tripoli, and Algiers swept the whole of the Mediterranean, penetrating to the North Sea and the Baltic; mutineers turned filibusters and buccaneers set up floating pirate states. And even the man who escaped these many perils might run the risk, as Lucae did between Speyer and Heidelberg, of being eaten alive by wolves.

216

Inns are described as very mediocre. Guarinonius complained that the German inns were dirty; Hainhofer, a travelled man, declared that Jüterbog offered the best lodging in Germany, and Misson, in 1687, while describing the Nuremberg inns as "quite unusually well appointed," could not be too caustic about the Italian ones, where six people were expected to satisfy their appetites on three eggs. It stood to reason that several travellers must expect to share a room, more often than not a bed. Pastor Hartmann gives us some inkling of the usual accommodation at inns when he expresses astonishment at finding in Wismar a guest-house with "so many small chambers that almost every guest could have one to himself." The question of gratuities was all-important. "Had to give the old wretch eight shillings," [1] notes Hartmann in his journal at Greifswald, and in Holland Lucae remarks, "Gratuities run away with even more money than board does, for the Dutch follow foreigners about for tips with perfectly shameless importunity."

Before high society confined its pleasure-seeking to Paris Italy, and Venice in particular, was the magnet of all who sought distraction. Count Frederick Christian of Schaumburg-Lippe, upon assuming the reins of government at the age of twenty-six, only treated Bückeburg as his temporary residence and spent at least half of his time in Italy. Dukes Ernest Augustus and George William of Hanover were little better. The latter wrote once to his court marshal, von Grapendorf, "I wish I could induce the marshal to come here, to stop him from perpetually writing to me to come home." These brothers gave entertainments costing between 7000 and 8000 thalers apiece, and even issued a bound volume, copiously illustrated with engravings, containing detailed descriptions of the regattas, pyrotechnical displays, and so forth held on these occasions. Of the saucy balls, such as the one organized by Mme de l'Isle d'Ayty, at which three hundred young girls danced *in puris naturalibus,* the Dukes unfortunately included no picture in their souvenir.

---

[1] The shilling (*Schilling*) was worth a thirty-second of a thaler (*cf.* p. 26, *n.* 4).

# INDEX

ABRAHAM A SANCTA CLARA, 126
*Acta Eruditorum,* 102
Adorno, Paolina, 49 *ill.*
Akersloot, Willem O., 55 *ill.*
Albert, Archduke of Austria, 31 *ill.*
Alcazar (Madrid), 69
Aldobrandini, family of, 81
Amling, Karl von, 203 *ill.*
Amstel, Adriaen Ploos van, 33 *ill.*
*Andromède* (Pierre Corneille), 96
Angermeier, Christoph, 78
Animal-baiting, 208
Anne of Austria, wife of Louis XIII, 53 *ill.*, 198, 209
Architecture, 64 *et seq.*, 86–88. *See also* Baroque architecture, Domestic architecture, Ecclesiastical architecture, French architecture, German architecture
Ariosto, Lodovico, 38, 94
Aristotle, doctrine of, 52
Arndt, Johann, 49
Art, 62 *et seq.*; collections, 79–81. *See also* Baroque art, Bologna, Dutch art, Dutch artists, English connoisseurs, French artists, French classicism, German art, German artists, Handcraftsmen, Interior planning, Landscape painting
*Artamène* (Madelène de Scudéry), 38, 191
Arundel, Thomas Howard, second Earl of, 81, 82
Aschaffenburg, Castle of, 66, 68
*Assassin,* 158
Astronomy, 53
Augsburg, 26, 77, 83, 133
Avercamp, Hendrick, *plate facing p.* 30, 41 *ill.*

BACHAUMONT, FRANÇOIS DE, 191
*Badin,* 158
Balde, Jakob, 196
Ballet, 93 *et seq.*
Barberini, Cardinal Antonio, 94
Barberini family, 81
Barelli, Agostino, 66

*Barett,* 124
Baroque architecture, 64 *et seq.*; art, 62 *et seq.*, 88
Bas, Elizabeth Jacobsz, 145 *ill.*
*Basse-lisse* tapestry, 78 *n.*
Batiste, 116, 131, 135
Baur, Johann Wilhelm, 37, 62 *ills.*
Bausch, Lorenz, 52
Beauchamps, —, 210
Bed-furnishings, 75
Bedford, William Russell, fifth Earl of, 130 *ill.*
Bedford, Countess of, 191
Bérain, Jean, 197 *ill.*
Berlin, 26, 72, 74, 78, 79, 90, 133, 170, 205, 208, 213; royal palace in, 70
Bernini, Giovanni Lorenzo, 65, 69, 87–88, 91
Besserer, Maria Martha, 184 *ill.*
Bissari, Count Pietro, 97, *n.* 1
Black dress, 135–136
Bloteling, Abraham, 192 *ill.*
Blount, Thomas, 144
Bodice, 128, 130 *et seq.*, 152, 154, 156
Bol, Ferdinand, 106 *ill.*
Bologna, School of, 66, 82
Bolswert, Scheltius van, 157 *ill.*
Bombasine, 156
Bombasting, 105, 130–131
Bonnart, —, 200, 201, 204, 205, 208 209 *ills.*
Bontekoe, Corneille, 203
Boot-hose, 145, *n.* 1
Borghese family, 81
Borromini, Francesco, 65
Bosse, Abraham, 57–59, 83, 84, 92, 109, 111, 113, 115, 117, 119–121, 123, 125 *ills, plates facing pp.* 128, 136, 142, 150, 163 *ill.*
Bossuet, J.-B., 60
Bostel, Lukas von, 98
Bourbon-Condé, Princesse de, 191
Brabant, Henning, 54–55
Brant, Isabella, 23 *ill.*
Breeches, 105, 114, 137, 138, 139, 140–142, 148
Briot, Isaac, II, 57, 60, 61, 63 *ills.*

219

# INDEX

# INDEX

# INDEX

# INDEX

227